DRAFT

You Won't Believe What Your Child is Thinking

To all children, everywhere

Acknowledgements

First and foremost, I want to thank the young clients—preschoolers through college students—who shared what they were thinking as they talked about their lives. Their surprising perspectives became the foundation for this book, which I hope will help other young people and families. Thank you also to the parents, teachers, and other adults who care about kids and dedicate their time and resources to helping our precious young people.

Another wave of gratitude goes to the friends and colleagues who helped this text come to life by sharing stories, giving feedback, proofreading, and believing in the project. The list of helpers includes Doretta Hale, Claire Thorpe, Megan Barber, Corky Morse, Gigi Eakins, Marcia Hope, Joelle North, Judy Piper, Brenda Joy Bratt, Karin Jacobson, Michelle Beaudreau, Don Linder, and Galen Garwood as interior and cover designer. Peggy Pace gave the world Lifespan Integration, which has changed the lives of my clients from 2 to 90 years old. Thank you, Peggy.

I extend deep appreciation to my family—Craig, David, Tim, and Kelly. Thanks for your support and for living out the power of being yourselves. You each turned out okay even though I didn't know then what I know now. And to someone very special who believed in me from the beginning and dared me to be an engine, "Thanks, Mom."

Cathy

You Won't Believe What Your Child is Thinking
© Catherine Thorpe 2019
Timeline Press
PO Box 53473,
Bellevue, WA 98015.

ISBN: 978-0-9819137-1-1

You Won't Believe What Your Child is Thinking, set in Adobe Caslon Pro, was designed by Galen Garwood.

You Won't Believe
What Your
Child is Thinking

Catherine Thorpe, MA

Timeline Press

CONTENTS

Introduction

After many years of interacting with young people as a parent and psychotherapist, I am astounded by the ways kids perceive their situations and what they believe about themselves as a result. In a phrase, the title of this book is the purpose of this book: to tell parents, caregivers and other adults *you won't believe what your child is thinking.* Most adults assume kids perceive situations the way adults perceive them, but I have discovered youngsters do not think in the ways we assume they do. What young people think is surprising—it is innocent, uninformed, frightening at times, and intuitive based on their environments, their natural gifts and what has been told to them. Kids think in these surprising ways because they are young and unsophisticated. This book is my effort to communicate to adults what young people of all ages often believe about themselves and to offer healing ideas for adults who interact with kids.

Day after day in my counseling practice young people tell me what they believe in their young minds. Similarly, adults tell me the thoughts and beliefs they held as children. For example, an adult client told me her father had a good job when she was growing up, but they bought all of her clothing at a second-hand store. Because of this, the client genuinely believed that other parents valued their children more than her parents valued her. Did anyone help this youngster understand why her parents, who had money, only purchased used clothing for their children? No. The client who told me this story was in her thirties and had never once re-evaluated her childhood belief. She had not reconsidered the assumption she made about her value based on where her parents bought her school clothes.

A more painful example of childhood thinking came from nine-year-old Rodrico who shared an experience of going to the zoo with his father. Rodrico's father, who was often violent with him, picked the child up and threatened to feed his son to the lions as he held him over the lion's exhibit.

"Did you believe him?" I asked.

The boy solemnly nodded his head yes.

"Did you think you would die?" I asked sincerely.

Once again, Rodrico solemnly nodded yes.

Rodrico had good reasons to believe what his father was saying. The threat inside this terrifying experience added to the Post-Traumatic Stress Disorder (PTSD) that brought him to my office. As a nine-year-old who had experienced abuse from his father, Rodrico did not have any way to understand his circumstance other than the concrete facts and words expressed by his dad. Sadly, these harsh words made a strong impression in his mind and formed his understanding of himself, others and the world.

What happens to young people is interpreted by young minds and becomes part of their thinking, regardless of the truth. The same parents who love and care for their kids also get fatigued and frustrated by them. Young people of all ages marinate in their caregiver's words, behaviors and daily emotions. This complex environment contributes to the way young people understand themselves. These right or wrong impressions form kids' ways of thinking about the world and specifically about themselves - a predicament of which most caregivers are unaware. I was certainly not conscious of this concrete version of young people's thinking until I began to work with them in psychotherapy. When I asked my own adult children if what I was learning in my practice was correct, they answered yes. I could hardly believe what they told me!

Adults and children form true and erroneous beliefs about themselves based on their conditions and the way they are treated in relationships. On a daily basis, people filter life's interactions and develop beliefs about themselves as a result. Young people are especially prone to using life situations as a feedback loop about themselves. They start to think, *I am bad* because they are treated badly, or *I don't matter* when they are neglected and abused, and *I am valuable because I am good at gymnastics* or *I help by taking care of others*. In the transition to adulthood, many young people interrupt this inclination and start to bring adult thinking to their lives. Adults may learn to override the tendency to define themselves by their environments, but young people often form ways of thinking about themselves through their accumulated experiences. These internalized beliefs can last a lifetime.

The first part of this book is about what young people think, how they came to believe it, and ways adults can compassionately help reshape erroneous ideas. Section One includes: 1) How everyone's thinking makes sense to them; 2) Four major components of faulty thinking for young people; 3) Expanded categories of what children believe; 4) How caregivers can understand and influence youngsters to think correctly; 5) Trauma's effect on beliefs and 6) The science behind thinking.

The first section will be valuable to adults who have regular interactions with kids. As mentioned, I was astonished when young people began to tell me how they were making sense of their worlds. I observed that they carried their erroneous beliefs forward and made repeated decisions based on inaccurate assumptions. Understanding the power of these right and wrong belief systems is important to know because beliefs underlie the actions, self-perceptions and self-worth of people everywhere.

The second section of the book entitled, *Perspectives*, reflects viewpoints I have developed interfacing with young people and their families over several decades. Many of the perspectives mentioned here will be good reminders of common practices. Some will be new tools to help adults find out what young people are thinking in order to help them and a few ideas will stand in contrast to current culture. On some issues my ideas are outside contemporary norms, but I propose these views believing they reflect the needs of young people and their unique requirements for mental, emotional and relational growth. For example, I propose Time In, not just Time Out, and I explain how this version of Time In can be a non-punitive way to help children calm down and engage well with others. The *Perspectives* section also includes outcomes from research that support a parenting style which sets children up for healthy self-esteem and effective interactions with others. Some parenting styles that hamper independence and success are also briefly mentioned.

The main form of therapy I use is Lifespan Integration (LI). LI is a professional counseling modality that helps people of all ages heal from their problems and think truthfully about themselves. I find Lifespan Integration heals gently and more quickly than talk therapy alone. It is a profound method for healing trauma, which does not re-traumatize clients or create secondary trauma for therapists. LI is used to heal a wide spectrum of issues, including birth trauma, adoption and various ways in which people become emotionally stuck and repeat dysfunctional patterns. Peggy Pace, MA, (2003) developed Lifespan Integration, which has become a mental health modality used around the world. I include a very brief case example in Chapter 6 on trauma, because it highlights the healing power and impact of LI. Changed thinking and behavior follow LI treatment.

Anyone who has a co-worker, friend, partner, or child knows someone with erroneous thinking. All humans are susceptible to leftover childhood misperceptions. Young people are especially vulnerable to misinterpreting themselves based on their environments. Some of the frustrations caregivers face are unwittingly based on kids' wrong thinking. When they discover what kids believe, parents, teachers and caregivers are in positions to help them understand the world correctly and develop healthy strategies. My goal through this book is to lighten life's journey for young people by informing adults about what kids believe and how adults can help them. Why is this important? *Because you won't believe what your child is thinking.*

Everyone's Thinking Makes Sense to Them

Chapter One
Everyone's Thinking Makes Sense to Them

Early in my counseling career, a seven-year-old taught me an unforgettable lesson that has become the title of this book. Joseph's parents brought him to my office because he was having anxiety about vomiting at school. He had never thrown up at school, but his fear about throwing up in class had become so problematic his family struggled every morning to get him ready and into his classroom. They brought him to counseling because they could not understand what was going on with Joseph.

Joseph's parents were eager to solve Joseph's fear of vomiting. In our first counseling session, they did most of the talking with Joseph present. They explained that the problem began at the end of second grade, but had worsened over the months, and was significantly impacting the family by the middle of third grade. There was no apparent reason for Joseph to have a fear of vomiting at school because he had never thrown up in any public setting. Joseph's parents described their son as a normal boy who met all the developmental stages on target. I found Joseph to be likable, although reserved, which is typical for many kids at a first meeting.

In our second session, I told Joseph we wanted to figure out what was going on inside of him that caused him to be afraid about throwing up at school. I gave him a choice of having his parents in the room. He decided to have his parents stay, but we agreed his parents would be excused if Joseph felt uncomfortable saying something he might not want his parents to hear. Joseph's parents agreed to the plan.

Bit by bit, Joseph began to reveal his worries about throwing up. At first, he could not name any reason or situation for his anxiety. We clarified there had never been a time when he felt even a little bit queasy at school. Joseph eventually said, "Well, there was one time at home, in the night, when I threw up."

"Tell me about that time," I encouraged.

Joseph explained how he had awakened in the middle of the night and felt sick. He went into his parents' bedroom about 2 am and stood at his dad's bedside. Then Joseph suddenly got very quiet. He looked at each of his parents uncomfortably and paused.

"Do you want me to ask your mom and dad to step outside now?" I asked gently, wanting to keep our conversation moving forward.

"No," he answered, quietly.

"Remember, we have an agreement you can say anything in front of your mom and dad." I replied.

Joseph silently looked at them again with concern.

"Your mom and dad want to help you, so please try to tell us what happened next," I added.

After a long, quiet pause, Joseph tenderly said, "I woke up my dad and told him I felt sick. He said, 'You'll be fine. Go back to bed.' I went back to my room and laid down in my bed. Then all of a sudden I threw up on everything." Joseph paused and anxiously looked back and forth between his parents again. "And that's when I knew I couldn't trust my dad anymore."

The feeling in the room deepened with Joseph's intimate confession of loss. He had told us his difficult, long-held secret of broken trust with his father. Joseph idolized his dad as many children do, and his father's comment, "Go back to bed, you'll be alright," turned out wrong. With such a confusing message, Joseph's young brain came to the conclusion he could not trust his dad.

Once we knew the heart of the situation, I moved toward helping Joseph understand the situation was over. Using therapeutic techniques, I helped Joseph process the misunderstanding. I observed shifts on a mental and bodily level. At the end of the session, Joseph seemed quite relieved to have shared the secret he was carrying in his heart. I felt the joy and intimacy return between Joseph and his parents.

I asked Joseph, "What happens right now when you think about going to school tomorrow? Do you feel afraid you might throw up?"

"No," Joseph answered. "Now I know it was just a mistake. How could my dad know if I was going to throw up or not?"

"Good point," I validated.

Joseph's parents left our second session relieved; Joseph left our session with his heart reunited with his father. A break in trust with his dad was the source of his vomiting anxiety. It is common for anxiety to appear to be about one cause yet be related to other factors. For Joseph, the anxiety he had been struggling with for months resolved when we identified the break in trust beneath the anxiety symptoms and resolved it. Joseph ended our session quite confident he would not feel anxious about throwing up the next day at school.

When Joseph and his parents came back the following week for a third session, Joseph reported that he had not experienced any anxiety about vomiting at school. It had been a good week for him. His parents described Joseph as the boy they knew before the problem had begun. At the end of our session, I told them they could call me for another appointment if the problem reoccurred. Six months later, Joseph's mother left a voicemail saying things continued to go well and Joseph showed no signs of anxiety about throwing up at school.

Fogel summarizes the essence of what happened for Joseph: An event occurs and our minds interpret the event to mean that *something is wrong;* then our minds draw a lesson from it about how we should act in the future, and the lesson becomes part of our programming.

The programming that follows events—whether it is accurate or inaccurate—continues to run, unchecked, for years after it was written. The mind uses its programming to interpret and respond to events long after the initial programming takes place. This is why everyone's thinking makes sense to them. In many cases, a person's internalized thoughts and beliefs can make sense to others, too, when they are understood from the same perspective.

Joseph was the first child in my professional life who confirmed my awareness that adults are often unaware of the ways young people think. Decades of parenting also set my mind in motion on this topic. Now when parents contact me about bringing their children to counseling, I tell them, "You might be surprised what this is about." So far, my experience has confirmed that young people are troubled about different things than adults, and kids of all ages perceive their worlds differently than parents can imagine. One of the first steps in counseling kids is to name their perspectives on a problem. Sometimes understanding the young person's perspective and speaking to it directly can be enough to help resolve their concern. At other times, resolving a youngster's distress is much more complex and needs more extensive therapy.

THE POWER OF THINKING

William James, the father of American psychology, once said, "Thinking is the grand originator of our experience." Every understanding in life is based on thought, including unconscious thinking and perception. Apart from the autonomic nervous system that regulates the body, human behavior is controlled by thinking. What we say, do, interpret and believe is a direct result of how we perceive situations. Perception is influenced by culture, family, and individual experience. Collectively and individually, perception leads into patterned systems of thinking, which governs whole societies.

History shows us how powerfully beliefs drive behavior. The following are three well-known, brief examples of cultural thinking which seem preposterous to us today, but in their time were believed and acted upon by whole societies. I cite them to underscore that thinking comes before behavior and children are not the only ones to misunderstand their worlds and act erroneously.

In 1431, the French national heroine Joan of Arc was condemned to death as a witch and was burned at the stake in France. The Christian church put to death about 300,000 women fopracticing witchcraft from 1484 to 1782. A witch was identified by the presence of moles, scars, or other marks on a woman's body-where a pin could be stuck without causing pain. During the 1600's and 1700's an almost hysterical fear of witchcraft swept most of Europe.

4

Christopher Columbus, one of the greatest explorers and navigators of all time, sailed from Spain in 1492. At the time, Europeans believed the earth dropped off at the end of the visible sea. They did not know that lands and people existed beyond their geographical realm. They believed Columbus and his men were sailing to their deaths when they launched from Spain.

Martin Luther King Jr. lost his life trying to influence a society's way of believing about race and human equality. His work to shift society's way of thinking in mid-century America brought resistance, riots, and death because individuals were dedicated to their current beliefs and lived those beliefs as if they were inherently true.

These three examples convey that whole societies have made heinous choices based on their erroneous forms of thinking. Thinking is so intrinsic that we learn to trust our thinking as reality, when in fact, thinking can be inaccurate and our assumptions incorrect. Behavior results from what we believe and has conscious and unconscious thinking at its root.

Why is this subject important for our precious young people? Adults are often puzzled by kids' actions because they do not know what kids are thinking—yet everyone's thinking makes sense to them. If we had insight into our children's thinking, we could help them grow in the world with love, understanding, and greater self-acceptance. We could influence their behavior with truth instead of the erroneous assumptions and decisions they make about themselves and others.

Most adults who care for young people have good intentions. They want youngsters to grow up to be safe and successful. In many cases, parents want their children to have better lives than their own, so they work hard to give them the best they have to offer. Yet young people absorb inaccurate ways of thinking even in the most optimum environments.

Thinking governs life. Changing beliefs often changes behavior; yet there is a caveat to this truth. Thinking occurs on many levels of the mind-body system. Making a decision to change one's intellectual thinking does not necessarily change the many years, and many layers, of thought systems which a person has come to absorb over a lifetime. Domestic violence is an example of multiple layers of internal thought systems. A perpetrator can attend a year's worth of domestic violence courses and become violent again when prompted by a circumstance which some part of the mind-body brain considers threatening. When the violent act is over, the individual may be puzzled by their own behavior. A violent response to a perceived threat is an example of thinking that comes automatically from part of the mind-body system, overriding a year's worth of intentional learning. Belief systems are much deeper than ideas to which one gives intellectual assent.

When I teach Lifespan Integration or speak to adults about kids' ways of thinking, I begin with a set of toddler's nesting cups in my hand. I hold up the first small cup and say, "This is how people are formed. In the womb, they form neural networks which load their experiences about life while in utero and during their births. If a birth was traumatic, the child's mind and body will remember it, and defend against reminders of the trauma, just like any other Post-Traumatic Stress Disorder (PTSD).

"As children grow, their bodies develop and their brains continue to process and load everything in their environments." I hold up the next little nesting cup and say, "One-and two-year-olds are laying down neural networks that remain in their bodies for life."

I continue stacking the cups one by one, eventually showing the collection of ten cups tucked inside one another. "People are a collection of selves just like this, and the thoughts, feelings and experiences throughout their lives are still inside them, influencing how they think and behave every day."

To conclude the example, I turn the cup over so only the largest cup is showing on the outside. "This is what people, including children, look like when we interact with them, but the person in front of us is actually made up of all these thoughts, feelings, and experiences," which I indicate by turning the nesting set over again so all the colorful cups can be seen tucked inside one another. "The experiences and beliefs people have collected throughout their lives don't go away, and there is no occasion when we dump out the contents of our cups. What we experience, we learn about and use to form beliefs about ourselves and the world—most of which stays inside us. The people we meet and interact with are actually like this on the inside," I indicate by showing ten cups inside one another, "but on the outside, they look like this—whole and complete." I demonstrate the appearance of wholeness by showing the outer cup without evidence of the other nine rings which make up its contents.

The nesting cup demonstration points out that sometimes we respond to life with our two-year-old mindsets, our teenager thinking and feeling, or our adult minds with little choice over which 'self' or inner cup reacts at a given time. Trauma memories get first priority because the human species is wired to keep itself safe. Even trauma memories can seem like reasonable adult perspectives, but actually be unconscious reactions from childhood traumatic experiences. For example, I see parents who control their teenagers based on their own teenage histories, without awareness that their teen is a very different person and lives in a different environment than the one in which the adult was raised. We are a composite of selves—a collection of all our life experiences—and current thinking comes from the summation of what we have experienced and believed throughout our lives.

An adult male once said to me over dinner, "My father was an alcoholic, but it didn't affect me at all." In my clinical practice a male client said, "Both of my parents were alcoholics and I knew I was worthless." Both of these men were wrong. They are both good people who have been affected by alcoholism. Their internal 'selves,' or collective cups, could not resist being shaped by the thoughts, feelings, and behaviors which occurred in their environments of alcoholism.

The first man erroneously believed it had no effect on him, but he over-responds to situations by yelling and controlling. His inappropriate behavior reflects a need to over-manage life and others because his childhood environment was chaotic and unsafe due to his parent's alcoholism.

The second man used his interactions with two alcoholic parents to draw erroneous conclusions about himself, resulting in low self-esteem. He relies on the thinking of a younger child inside him to determine his value in the present. His parents were unable to reflect an accurate sense of his inherent value to him due to their own challenges, which led him to avoid people and opportunities that could have been positive influences in his life. Believing he was worthless shaped his vocation and academic choices.

Culturally and personally we live what we believe, even if we don't agree with our own actions. As mentioned, what people think and believe is so integral to them that whole societies chart their courses based on accepted views and beliefs. Countries go to war over differing ideas yet as global thinking changes, communities and cultures change as well.

Thought helps us make sense out of the world; it shapes our reality from the inside out. Our thinking is an attempt to interpret situations and form an internal response, which generates behavior. Carlson writes, "Ultimately, the relationship you have to your own thinking will determine your mental health and happiness." As William James purported, thinking is the beginning of our emotional and behavioral life experience. Perception, accurate or not, leads to patterns of thinking, which are laid down in the human mind and body as programs for life.

MICHAEL OHER'S STORY

Michael Oher's story is a first-hand account of a child's perspective on parents and the innate attachment to family. His journey from childhood poverty to the NFL is portrayed in the book and movie *The Blind Side*. Today Oher owns a Super Bowl ring, but his life started as one of 12 children born to a drug-addicted mother. He grew up unsupervised in government housing projects without sufficient food, electricity, and water. Yet Oher's siblings worked very hard to stay together and repeatedly ran away from various foster homes. At one time seven of them lived in a car without their mother for a month. He writes, "I loved my brothers and sisters so much that I was always determined to look out for them and wanted to live as near to them as I could."

Oher and his siblings lived in physical and emotional deprivation yet one of their highest priorities was maintaining family cohesiveness and protecting one another. Authorities attempted to place the children in safe environments, but they resisted adult intervention. Their view reflects the thinking of kids and is not congruent with the adult perspective that children need safe supervision and care.

How could safety, food, and genuine care be resisted by young people who organically need these things? We miss an important viewpoint if we don't take into account how the world seems to youngsters, and the degree to which they innately love their biological families. Children and pets are the unconditional lovers on our planet. Even when neglected, abused and mistreated, kids often hold a genuine love in their hearts for their families. They can have a mythical love for a parent with whom they have very little contact and adopted children long for their 'real' moms and dads. It is important to keep this in mind when we help young people through the process of separation from their families of origin. The ways young people prioritize families and relationships are very different than adults who prioritize the needs to keep children safe, housed, and fed.

We can help young people resolve emotional conflicts in their hearts and minds about circumstances over which they had no control when we give them appropriate, honest information. In scenarios like those mentioned above, we can begin to mitigate the effects of trauma for young people by understanding how they interpreted situations to be about themselves. We can view circumstances from the lens of concrete, cause-and-effect young thinkers and offer them other ways to understand situations which validate their perspectives and lighten their loads.

I have often said to a young client, "Everybody loves their mom and it makes sense you want to be with her. Right now, there's a rule that says she can only be with you if she keeps you safe, and she hasn't figured out how to do that yet. This probably doesn't seem fair because you want to be with your mom so much, but there's nothing about you that has made this happen. You are a good kid and this is a tough situation."

A positive exhale usually follows with a response such as, "I never thought about it like that...." Most young people in difficult situations have some degree of belief that if they had been better things would have turned out differently for them. As cause-and-effect thinkers, young people believe they must have done something wrong to warrant their current situations. Kids of all ages have young thinking and do not know what adults presume they know. Obviously, I don't know every child and therefore I can't speak for all of them yet I am reporting general trends I see regarding how many youngsters think about themselves and others—all the way into their twenties.

One way we can help young people grow into their potential is to help them identify the thinking beneath their behavior. It may take a bit of maneuvering to find out what kids are thinking, but when we do, we can help relieve distress at its source. Children can act one way if they read the environment to mean they are good; and act another way if they interpret the environment to mean they are bad. The beliefs *I am good* or *I am bad* lead to different responses and life choices long after circumstances are over. Restated, kids who believe they are inherently good, but make mistakes, act one way, and youngsters who believe they are inherently bad act differently. This does not mean we have to alter how we raise children so they never feel remorse, sadness, or regret. It does mean we are wise to discover what young people believe about themselves so we can help them sift through these beliefs and retain healthy ones.

Caregivers are living dialysis machines which help kids process and make sense of their worlds. A dialysis machine does externally what a patient's body cannot do on its own. Like this important machine, adults can intercept and correct the erroneous ideas young people gather about themselves from their environments and return to them a healthier form of understanding. Many of a young person's erroneous beliefs are based on the feelings and distress of others. When we deliberately ask kids what they are thinking in various situations, we can clarify their perceptions and provide them with accurate information for maneuvering through life.

Adults giving accurate information to children can change the course of their lives. An adult client shared how her mother pre-empted a bad form of thinking for her in the midst of a difficult situation in her teen years. The client's father came to a basketball game drunk in the small community where she went to high school. The referee stopped the game and confronted her father. At half time the client hid herself in shame. She said to me, "I did not know why my dad was drunk, but I tied my self-worth to his embarrassing behavior. When I told my mother about it she said, 'Fortunately, people don't hold these things against children.'"

The client reported that her mother's words instantly gave her relief because they changed her wrong thinking. Instead of being ashamed of herself and believing she was disqualified from membership in her peer group the next day at school, the teen shifted to believing she was acceptable in spite of her dad's drunkenness. The client said, "Because I believed my mother, I went to school on Monday, and every day thereafter, understanding that my father's alcoholism was not a reflection of me. I would not have known this without my mom directly telling me."

In some cases, like this teen's story, an adult's words are sufficient to re-orient a young person's thinking from an erroneous belief and behavior to the truth. Joseph's story, which opened the chapter, is another example of change occurring from simply identifying a young person's erroneous belief and correcting it. Because a person's belief system includes the collective scope of their mind, some ways of thinking may only change with therapeutic interventions.

Because the way young people think is inherently tied to their behavior, I seek to understand how kids understand themselves and their situations when I counsel them. I also work to understand what is most distressing to young clients and what they are thinking within the distress. When we find what troubles kids, and identify their thinking, we are halfway toward a solution. The other half of the solution lies in helping a youngster believe the truth in such a way that it transforms their behavior. More than a brief statement may be required to correct a young person's belief because thinking patterns become established throughout a child's collective years and are stored in the body. The body's neural firing system is the storehouse for thinking. Chapter six—*The Science Behind Believing*—lays a foundation for understanding how young people arrive at some of their beliefs.

Chapter Two

What Children Believe

When I begin working with a new family regarding their son's or daughter's distress, I tell parents over the phone, "You might be surprised what this is about." I make this comment because I have found it to be true over and over again. Adults often assume kids think the way adults think. Yet young people's perceptions can be very different than that of their caregivers. Often youngsters are not mature or informed enough to perceive situations correctly, they are sometimes directly given misinformation, they form their own ways of thinking based on the emotional, subjective aspects of an experience, and occasionally kids are right and grownups are wrong.

FOUR PRINCIPLES

Four general principles regarding what young people correctly or incorrectly come to believe are listed below:

1. Young people perceive the world with themselves at the center.
From this self-centered position, they use cause-and-effect thinking to make sense of their worlds, which often means *I caused it.*

2. Young people take words at face value.
They believe what they are told, which means *I believe it.*

3. Young people are prone to form "*I am...*" beliefs as a result of their experiences.

Converting an experience into one's identity means, *I personalize it.*

4. Young people develop strategies in response to their situations.

Their strategies become life-long patterns, which means *I adapt to it.*

I caused it, I believe it, I personalize it and I adapt to it can apply to people of all ages yet they are the hallmark of understanding the world for many kids. Toddlers through adults interact with the world via these lenses, and young people are especially prone to interpret what happens around them to be in some way about them. A college student's story portrays these four principles.

Star was between her second and third year of university when she came for counseling. "I don't think I'm going to make it through college," she said. "I used to be intelligent, but now I'm almost failing out of school."

Star began recounting her story. Through middle school, Star had been an outstanding student who was well liked by her peers. She played on the volleyball team and was president of her class.

"But, I had a boyfriend starting in eighth grade and that's when things really began to change," Star said. "My mom and stepdad were fighting a lot and I thought one of the best things I could do to help them was to stay out of the way. My stepdad and I fought regularly and sometimes my parents fought over stuff about me. I figured since I was part of the problem, I could be part of the solution by being gone as much as possible. I stopped coming home at night to give them and myself a break. I got pregnant when I was in ninth grade and had an abortion without telling my parents. I had another abortion two years later. I didn't tell them about that one either. I felt so bad about the abortions, and how my life was going, I started using drugs and alcohol. I got involved with a drug-using group at school and stopped doing my homework. I got cut from the volleyball team because my grades were so bad and I went from being an 'A' student to a 'D' student."

"What did you think about yourself when things were changing like that?" I asked.

"Not very good," Star answered.

"Would you say *I am bad* fit your story, or something else?"

"Oh, *I am bad* definitely fits my story," Star confirmed, "along with *I am a failure, I am irresponsible, I can't be trusted* and a whole lot of other things."

"What did people tell you when this was going on?" I asked.

"My stepdad used to say things to me like, 'You used to be smart, but now you're irresponsible and lazy.' He said I couldn't be trusted."

"Did you believe him?" I asked.

"Of course," Star answered, "it was true."

"How did you cope with the abortions?" I asked.

"I never told anyone but my boyfriend about them," Star replied. "It was right after the second abortion that my grades started to slide. I feel really bad that I had the abortions, but I didn't know what else to do as a junior in high school."

"And then the drug-use got worse, is that right?" I asked.

"Yes," she replied, "I was confused, I was having trouble concentrating in class and people didn't like me the same way anymore. I could tell that my teachers didn't like me as much either. My parents were no help."

"It sounds like you did not have a place to offload some very hard stuff and you tried to emotionally separate yourself through drugs and other ways of creating emotional distance." I explained dissociation to Star as an attempt to get emotional and mental distance from difficulties we can't solve. Dissociating is the primary defense children use when they are powerless to make things better in their circumstances. It is an attempt to not feel, think, or be fully present to something difficult.

Star agreed that drugs and alcohol were her ways to dissociate.

"Do you find yourself dissociating now?" I asked.

"Absolutely!" she answered, "I can't get back to being a responsible, good student. My mind doesn't work in the same way anymore."

15

Star attended many months of counseling, which focused on helping her resolve the angst that was still in her body-mind about the abortions and other choices she made in high school. Star made decisions based on young thinking, which included messages from her childhood environment. Our work centered on getting her back to something close to 'factory reset' for her inherent personality and gifts. Star's story is an example of the four components that are common to many young people:

1) Star viewed the world with herself at the center and used cause-and-effect thinking to interpret what was happening around her.

Star genuinely believed she was no longer smart and was part of the reason her mother and stepfather did not get along. Like her mother, Star also fought with her stepdad. As she described his personality to me, I suspected many people would have trouble relating to him. Yet Star saw the situation in her house with herself in the center and did not use broader thinking to assess why she and her mother were often in conflict with her stepdad. Her thinking included *I caused this.*

2) Star took her stepdad's words at face value when he said she was a failure, irresponsible, untrustworthy and no longer smart.

Once they were stated, Star accepted her stepdad's remarks as permanent personality traits. When I met Star, she seemed very intelligent, was finishing a college degree and had a good track record for work. Star may have been faltering in several areas during adolescence, which can happen to teens, but her stepfather's assessments of Star were not a truthful foundation for building her sense of self. Yet Star's reaction to her stepdad's behavior was *I believe this.*

3) Star combined her stepdad's words with her own insecurities and developed negative *I am* beliefs about herself.

Because Star used her stepdad's reactions as a mirror for her identity, Star surmised with a young mind that she was a person of little value, which she translated into *I personalize this.* She believed *I am bad, I'm a failure, I can't succeed, I have a broken mind* and other negative ideas. Star's *I am* beliefs affected her outcomes long after adolescence.

4) Star developed strategies in response to her situation. Eventually, her strategies took on a life of their own.

After the abortions, Star began to use drugs and alcohol to manage her thoughts and feelings. Substance abuse and dissociation became her strategies for coping with situations Star did not know how to address. Poor academic performance and truancy from school were strategies that matched her *I am* beliefs, which unfortunately reinforced a negative view of herself.

When Star began counseling, more than five years after her first abortion, each of the above internal programs was still running and contributing to her poor performance in college. It became clear early in her therapy that Star still considered herself bad, irresponsible and a failure. She had not been able to find a way to turn around these ways of thinking even though she had outgrown her middle school and high school behaviors. Star's collective thinking made sense to her. Our work focused on addressing each of the four elements that set Star on an erroneous understanding of herself, which reflected in her inability to perform well in college. Today she holds a Master's Degree and is a school principal.

These four components briefly illustrated with Star's story apply to many kids. These principles are developed more fully in the following sections.

PRINICPLE ONE—*KIDS PERCEIVE THE WORLD WITH THEMSELVES AT THE CENTER; THEY USE CAUSE-AND-EF-FECT THINKING TO UNDERSTAND THEIR WORLDS.*

For youngsters, life is a feedback loop of learning. What they experience, they turn into meaning, and often meaning about themselves. This statement might surprise adults who know that kids generally do not cause life's circumstances. Yet young people do not think like adults, they think like kids.

Young people start life from the vantage point of themselves in the center, and important others are like planets rotating around them. In earlier years of scientific discovery, humans believed the sun rotated around the earth because observable, concrete evidence suggested it was true. Youngsters use the same observable, but erroneous, cause-and-effect thinking to make sense of their worlds. They view life from their vantage points and fit others' words and behaviors into their frames of reference. Kids cannot know what is true until they have developed enough complexity to see the world from more than one vantage point. Until then, they use concrete, observable data to decipher the world. They are prone to consider events and people around them as elements inside their worlds and not as separate, external people and circumstances.

For example, one of my clients, Susan, described the way her mother's personality traits became merged with her own identity. Initially, Susan was the planet around whom her mother revolved. Eventually, the mother used the child's natural dependence to draw her daughter into an exclusive relationship for the mother's benefit. As an older child and teen, Susan took care of her mother who presented herself as weak, afraid and dependent. Well into young adulthood, Susan believed she would cause her mother to fail if she moved out of her stabilizing, central position. Such is the burden of self-at-the-center with cause-and-effect thinking. Young people can naturally hold these types of perspectives, but ideally outgrow these viewpoints and develop more mature living over time.

In many cases, young people assume they have had some part in creating what they experience because they can only see the world from their perspectives. They can be very concrete thinkers and interact with the world in a simple cause-and-effect fashion, as mentioned.

It is not uncommon for kids to believe that a condition, event or problem is in some way caused by them, even if it is not. Cause-and-effect thinking means *if it happened, I caused it, or it's about me.* If an experience is unpleasant, they may tie the event to what they did or did not do to make the difficult circumstance occur. Kids' brains do not have the sophisticated levels of development adult brains generally have, and therefore they cannot think like adults in similar situations.

Not all children turn every event into a personal problem, but all people learn from life experiences and there is no time when human brains stop downloading and interpreting information coming at them. With age and maturity, many older children and adults move beyond simplistic ways of cause-and-effect thinking. Unfortunately, many individuals continue this behavior well into adulthood.

An adult's story from childhood portrays the same concept. Marco was eight years old when he spent several weeks at his grandparents' home because his parents were divorcing. Marco rarely received physical comfort from any of his caregivers, but one night, while he laid in bed blinking his eyes at the overhead light, his grandmother came in and gave him a rare goodnight kiss. Every night thereafter Marco blinked at the light, hoping it would cause his grandmother to come and kiss him again. Unfortunately, he only received one bedtime kiss while he stayed with his grandparents, but he blinked at the light every night for the duration of his time there. Marco's young mind correlated blinking with hugs —a child's typical cause-and-effect perspective.

When I help young people identify their thoughts and feelings, I often discover that they have internalized events to be about themselves as cause-and-effect thinkers. They have not given thought to what it might be like to be the other person in the situation, whose behavior and words are driven by factors apart from the child. Kids' thinking is often, *I probably caused what happened,* to which they add a value judgment about themselves. For example, if a youngster is spoken to with an angry voice, the young person often believes they caused the anger and may add a value judgment about themselves, such as *I'm no good.* Young people can be inclined to create judgements about their own identities more readily than add a value judgment about the other person. Not all young people have the sophisticated capacity to think *that grown-up is probably mad about something else; my dad must be stressed about work;* or *I can see that mommy is tired because the new baby kept her up last night.*

Even adults can be inclined to wrongly attribute another person's behavior to something about themselves. When a supervisor comes in grumpy, how many adults wonder if they did something to cause the supervisor's mood? Overriding this self-centric, cause-and-effect tendency is a developed skill of adulthood. Yet many adults retain this cause-and-effect thinking as an outgrown artifact of childhood belief systems.

PRINICIPLE TWO—*CHILDREN BELIEVE WHAT THEY ARE TOLD. THEY TAKE WORDS AT FACE VALUE.*

Kids believe what others tell them including stories about Santa Claus and the Tooth Fairy because adults tell them these fantasy characters are real. Adults derive pleasure from children believing in these benevolent myths. Individually and collectively, we pass these traditions from one generation to the next and most of us can remember a time when we thought gifts magically appeared. Young people accept these myths because adults and other kids give them reasons to believe. Young children especially do not have the sophistication or life experience to sift truth from fiction regarding the stories they hear. Years after people have outgrown myth believing, they continue to gain pleasure from passing on a myth like Santa Claus. Kids believe in false tales because they take at face value what they hear.

In North America, children are told that a Tooth Fairy comes at night to collect the baby teeth they lose as they grow up. This benign tradition instructs a child to place a tooth, which finally wiggled loose, under their pillow. Then the Tooth Fairy flies around the world each night, silently enters a child's room, stealthily removes the tooth from under the pillow, and leaves money in exchange for the tooth. Curiously, the Tooth Fairy leaves different amounts of money in different children's homes, which is a serious topic of discussion in lower grade classrooms. Even though children receive different amounts of money, and the Tooth Fairy tradition varies from household to household, children earnestly continue to believe in this well-loved creature.

This actual statement from a seven-year-old speaks to the earnestness of a child's capacity to believe what he has been told. A boy awakened his mother at her bedside one morning and forlornly said, "The Tooth Fairy didn't come last night."

"Oh, honey," she replied in a compassionate, but semi-awake state, "Don't you know I'm the Tooth Fairy?"

Aghast, he answered, "Is that why you are so tired every morning?"

Sometimes kids are given playful, mythical messages to believe like those about the Tooth Fairy; at other times perpetrators deliberately abuse a young person's willingness to believe in order to manipulate or take advantage of them. Erroneous information comes from many sources, including other kids. Young brains believe what is said to them because they generally have not developed filters to decipher the difference between truth, legends, threats, or false promises. As mentioned, young, developing brains operate in concrete thinking, therefore, they cannot reason as adults reason. Therefore, it is important to consider what children are thinking in order to build positive and constructive frameworks for their lives.

Myth-telling might be an enjoyable way to communicate cultural customs to a younger generation, but adults must treat this trust with care. Young people believe what they are told and can suffer at the hands of adults and others because they naturally believe the lies, threats, and manipulations they hear. Kids also believe the good things people say to them. Even if they are suspicious about the true nature of positive messages, youngsters cannot help but internalize the words others say to them. A young brain is very impressionable; truth and lies spoken by adults can be remembered for a lifetime. The following examples are positive and negative stories I have heard from young people and adults regarding what they heard and believed in childhood.

Eddie changed schools and told his father he was sad because he did not have any friends in his new school. His dad told him to make new friends. A few days later the father discovered that Eddie had attempted to make friends out of cardboard because his son had understood him to mean that he had to literally construct friends out of available materials.

Jeanine was told by her uncle that he would throw her out the second story window if she ever told anyone what he was doing to her. The uncle told Jeanine that she liked what was happening and if she ever told anyone about it, he would find her and follow through on his threat. This is the story of a 65-year-old client who has carried a terrified, lonely two-year-old inside herself for a lifetime. Jeanine very seldom feels safe in the world because her early life was an ongoing experience of PTSD.

21

Luke's mother was ready for her two-and-a-half-year-old son to stop drinking from his baby bottles so together they packed every bottle in the house and left them on the front steps for Santa Claus. The mother promised Luke that Santa would replace them with a gift. When it was time to go to bed, Luke lost his courage and asked to have his nighttime bottle, only to find a delightful present on the porch where his bottles had been. Miraculously, Santa had come unnoticed on a warm July evening.

High school sophomore Trevor was given the results of a skills and aptitude test. The guidance counselor told him he had high scores in every category, which meant he could be successful in any area that interested him. He, like many teenagers, had low self-confidence and the counselor's words enabled him to venture into areas of college education he would not have considered, based on his perception of himself. Reflecting back on this experience as an adult, Trevor attributed the extra courage he needed to pursue post-college education to the test outcome and the words of the guidance counselor.

A frustrated, shame-filled father told his twelve-year-old son, "Michael, you ruin everything you do! What's the matter with you?!" Michael wondered, *what is wrong with me?* Michael generated a lot of chaos and failure in his life thereafter. Even though he was a gifted person, Michael had very low self-esteem and sabotaged many of his successes, fulfilling his father's forecast into adulthood.

The list of words said to young people can go on and on. I cite a few of the phrases I have heard to underscore the point that children believe what they are told. Sometimes the words are playful or meant to be supportive; other times painful words are generated from an adult who is hurting and angry. Depending on their ages, kids are limited in their capacity to sort the truth about themselves out of the angry or frightened projections thrust on them. Kids generally don't think *I'm not really a failure at everything I do; my dad is just frustrated right now.* Young people do not have built-in filter systems to help them separate truth from fiction. Yet when adults take the time and effort to share positive words with kids, these remarks are often remembered as well. What young people hear becomes loaded into their neural networks and influences the way they live, love and perceive the world into adulthood. Therefore, it is important for adults to understand what kids are thinking in order to build positive and constructive frameworks for their lives.

The previous paragraphs represent conversations youngsters take at face value, but educational systems are also built on young people taking words as presented. Students throughout their 20's are expected to accept educational curriculums as taught. A great deal of education is built on young people believing as truth what they hear in classrooms and other forms of instruction. The nature of young people's openness to learning means they will receive ideas about history, mathematics, science, culture and the nature of the world by direct instruction, which they are expected to receive as presented. Some academic truths appear to be universal, but young people around the globe also receive influence in human roles, ethnic biases, theology, ideology and every other discipline. Students are rewarded when they reiterate what instructors have taught them. Learners of all ages are in a process which requires them, at least in part, to take at face value what they hear.

Finally, but not exclusively, cultural values are presented to young people outside the classroom as ideas to be accepted by caregivers and society at large. Specifically stated or not, young people are influenced by caregivers' values and behaviors. These forms of learning load into the neural networks of young people as presented and repeated. Just like kids speak the language of their households, young family members are trained in social behavior, racial biases, sexual roles, and income level standards. In a sense, these concepts are taken at face value as well—not because young people want to perpetuate the values of their caregivers, but because these ideas seep into the conscious and unconscious brains of young people as they live in their communities.

Inherently, young people are determining if they are valuable, lovable and capable through this multi-layered process of taking in data from their environments. Young people are inclined to take at face value their interpretation of the data coming at them, which may be positive or negative. Often, they do not have the sophistication or maturity to filter the messages, values and ideology of other people, so they end up receiving how the world presents itself to them through their twenties and beyond.

Children Do Not Seek Validation for What They Hear

Parents do not know what others have said to their kids or how young people have made meaning out of their experiences. You won't believe what your child is thinking because you probably don't know what young people have surmised or been told. Kids of all ages can believe what they hear without asking others to confirm it.

When I was a young adolescent, a pediatrician told me that if I kissed my elbow I could change from a girl into a boy or vice versa. I started puzzling on his comments right away. He was a doctor, which gave him credibility about the body, and my father favored the sons in our family. Right away I perceived the difficulty of accomplishing this feat, but something about it appealed to me, so I seriously mulled the doctor's comments over for many weeks. I did not ask my mother after the appointment if the doctor's idea was correct.

This benign anecdote belies a truth underneath most of the curious, odd, or frightening words spoken to young people. Kids do not fact check with others, in part, because they don't know they should confirm what has been said to them. When young children are told that wolves come out at night and eat kids who tell lies or don't brush their teeth, young children believe these words. Even if older kids suspect these ideas might be false, most messages create some degree of belief depending on a young person's age. Youngsters are newcomers to the world. Their life experiences are based upon the care and choices of adults; therefore, they have to accept how adults treat them and what adults say to them. Young people are accepting, and often not empowered enough to check the statements of one adult against another adult.

Young people do not vet what has been said to them for many reasons. The list of reasons includes: they are too young or naïve to know they should get corroborating support; they are shamed by what has been told to them and shame keeps them silent; they want to believe something they have heard; and they have been threatened to keep secrets. These are just a few of the motivations which prevent young people of all ages from finding out if what they have been told is true.

Why wouldn't kids naturally accept what they have heard? If we look at the world from their viewpoints, we can see that young people are learning new things in life almost every day. We ask them to take at face value what adults tell them. As discussed, young people are physiologically in rapid phases of development and learning. Adults tap into this accelerated capacity and educate children when they are young, bright and open. Yet this very openness makes young people vulnerable to believing whatever they are told without verifying one adult's information against another's.

My high school English teacher initially taught his toddler erroneous words for every object in their house, assuming the child would later learn the correct names for each object. He thought it was cute that his son pointed to the light and called it water, identified the toilet as a dog, and was told to sit on his turkey instead of his bottom. As a student in his classroom, I did not find my teacher's antics too clever, but his endeavor demonstrates a child's willingness to believe without corroboration.

Some young people take at face value what they are told rather than seek verification because they are threatened with serious consequences if they share what they are holding. Anisha mentioned a family concern to her school counselor who shared the comment with Anisha's mother who also worked for the school system. On the day her mother had the conversation with the school counselor, Anisha returned home from school to find a very angry parent who said, "Don't you ever tell other people what happens in this house!" Anisha clearly understood the larger message behind her mother's words, namely: *Keep our family secrets. We cannot let other people know what happens in our family. You are not allowed to seek outside help for our problems.* Exchanges like these influence young people to accept at face value what they hear.

Families are ripe environments for accepting untrue thoughts in young people's minds due to shame. If a mother says to her child, "Your father is leaving us because you are so annoying," the child will not ask the father if these words are true. The emotional tone and actual content of such a message will cause a child to feel shame and shame is not easily shared.

Shame messages imply an inherent lack of value. For example, if a student asks a genuine question which the teacher answers with sarcasm or belittlement, the student may experience a feeling of shame because the teacher's reply was a message about the student's stupidity in response to a genuine question.

Shame is one of the reasons kids do not corroborate one parent's word with another, the babysitter's remarks with mom when she gets home, or a stepparent's message with the other parent. Shame is one of the most excruciating emotions humans experience. People are unlikely to seek corroborating or clarifying information in fear they will find a shameful comment is true.

Teasing

Children under four years old almost always believe what others say to them, even if it is inaccurate. Kids as old as late adolescents may have trouble filtering sarcasm and double meanings, which adults often use for engaging young people. It may be fun for an adult or others to tease kids, but kids do not always grasp that a game is being played and the goal of the game is to understand a meaning other than the words being expressed.

I am not suggesting young people should never be playfully teased. Youngsters of all ages can easily enter into and understand playful banter with words and funny statements. Kids increase their emotional and social capacity when they are lovingly cued in the world of double meanings and word plays. Yet young children especially may take teasing at face value. Teasing may need to be interpreted by someone close to a young person or they will internalize erroneous and hurtful messages underneath the teasing. For example, kids have been told the mail carrier or someone else brought them to the family and if they are naughty the mail carrier can take them away. A comment like this may seem humorous to adults, but be taken seriously by a young person. The message within the intended humor is that the youngster's opportunity to stay within the family is based on whether they are good or bad and there are readily available ways to send them somewhere else. Is this too sensitive and overstated? Maybe. Do kids really think this way? Yes. They tell me they believed what others said to them, including that UFOs fly around in space and can remove them from their homes.

When adults understand how young people think about the 'harmless' things said to them, kids can be informed that a teasing game is being played. Often children will enter into the game once they understand what is happening and playful exchanges can go forward as something fun for both parties. I personally think we under-inform and over-assume what kids know regarding teasing. Teaching them how to field double-meanings is sometimes as simple as explaining what is happening and discovering how the young person is interpreting and handling it.

An elementary teacher reinforced this perspective. She playfully suggested a silly idea to her one of her students who looked confused and concerned. She read the expression on his face and said with a smile, "I'm joking."

He instantly relaxed and smiled in return.

"Oh, you're joking me," he said with relief.

Until the teacher explained that her clever comment was in jest, he took her playful words at face value and became noticeably distressed until she informed him about the nature of their exchange.

In summary, young people take words at face value because they are young. We can still use humor and double-meanings with young people, but it is helpful to keep in mind that depending on their ages, kids may not understand the true meaning or intent behind adult words. Some communication is meant to engage youngsters in cultural myths and traditions; some expressions help kids see themselves in a more truthful and positive light; and some comments hurt and confuse them. Without regard to the content, young people of all ages may internalize at face value some, or all, of the words spoken around them and most kids will initially inherit the customs and behaviors of their cultures as truth.

Educational venues often send messages young people are expected to accept and unconscious information is transferred within societies. Adults can intercept and correct the complex ways young people make interpretations of the world. These interventions can be direct, playful or subtle and still be effective.

PRINCIPLE THREE—*CHILDREN ARE PRONE TO FORM 'I AM...' BELIEFS AS A RESULT OF THEIR CIRCUMSTANCES*

All people, not just kids, tend to use circumstances and interactions as information about themselves. Young people are especially vulnerable to this tendency and ideas developed in childhood can last a very long time. Kevin's story reinforced this concept for me. As an adult, Kevin began to address an issue in counseling, which led us directly back to a childhood *I am* belief. Forty-two-year-old Kevin described his ongoing financial circumstances and I inquired about his *I am* belief.

"Would, *I am a failure* fit your sense of self in this experience?" I asked.

"Completely," he answered, subtly communicating *Of course, I am a failure; I just told you I'm not earning enough money.* In my mind, it was possible for many reasons to constitute financial challenges, but the undertone of Kevin's remarks clearly centered on his sense of self. As part of our Lifespan Integration work, I asked Kevin to focus on the core of his body to bypass his conscious thinking and to let his body-mind system take him to an earlier time in his life related to his current distress. The body-mind affect bridge is a powerful way of relying on the body to reveal truths the conscious mind may not easily retrieve.

Kevin opened his eyes and said, "I'm remembering the day when I was seven years old and our mother sat us down and said, 'It's better for you if I never see you again.'"

I was incredulous and confused. How could a woman think it was better for her children to never have contact with their mother again and how could this memory be connected to the idea *I am a failure*?

Because the body tells no lies, I knew something about the earlier memory was contributing to how Kevin conceptualized his financial problem. I asked him to explain. After Kevin gave more details about his childhood situation, I asked, "Does *I am a failure* fit the childhood situation?"

"Absolutely!" he answered. "I believed I was a failure as a kid or my mom wouldn't be leaving me. I failed to be the kind of person whose mom would want to stay."

As Kevin's case portrays, clients can follow the body-mind affect bridge to earlier memories, which reveals earlier core beliefs. Their current and younger *I am* beliefs invariably match one another. Children use young, immature thinking to understand their difficult experiences as something personal about themselves. Why is this so?

28

In combination with their natural personalities, young people develop a sense of self through their circumstances, how they are treated, and what they are told. Their overall, burgeoning identity is produced in the alchemy of these elements. *I am* beliefs result and can go on to influence their perceived self-value and self-identity for a very long time. As people age, ideally their maturity deepens and they gain greater capacity for understanding themselves from the inside out, rather than the simple cause-and-effect of external factors determining their worth. The factors mentioned here become stored as *I am* beliefs:

Circumstances

Children, and many adults, use the world as a house of mirrors which reflects back to them their sense of value and place. Parents, caregivers, peers and circumstances are life's mirrors for children. What young people observe in life's mirrors is often taken as true information about themselves. As we know, a house of mirrors can be very confusing because it includes distorted images. Even though life's house of mirrors is a poor source of identity, kids can use this information as determinants for how they see themselves. Undesirable physical traits, difficult living conditions, problems with parents, academics, athletics, etc. can become direct feedback about a young person's worth. We do not have to protect kids from life's real challenges, but it is important to know that young people are vulnerable to converting negative and positive circumstances into messages about themselves.

Treatment

How kids are treated equals their perceived self-value to a rather high degree. It is hard for young people to emerge from neglect with a positive sense of self, from abandonment believing they are worth keeping, and from verbal negativity with positive identities. Fortunately, the opposite is true as well. Positive treatment bolsters kids' self-worth and carries tremendous weight. The treatment young people receive affects how they see themselves in the present and generally transfers to the ability to care for themselves well later in life.

Words

Positive words and tones help young people absorb positive ideas about themselves. Even if children struggle to believe the affirming things adults tell them, words matter and have lasting influence beyond the moment when words are spoken. Young people tend to receive verbal messages as truth, especially if they are spoken with intensity. An angry parent stating, "What's the matter with you!?" leaves a strong, negative impression about identity in a youngster's mind. Similarly, encouraging, positive words leave a lasting impression as well. Words are a powerful force for helping kids understand themselves, whether positive or negative.

Innate Personality

Kids are born with natural personalities that cannot be parented out of them. From the beginning of their lives, young people have natural temperaments, which influence how they interpret situations and come to know themselves. For example, some kids encounter challenges and see them as problems to conquer, while other youngsters face obstacles and collapse due to feelings of inadequacy. These inborn personality traits, and success or failure at being themselves in the world, shape young people's views of themselves.

We cannot turn our kids into anything we want them to be. Caregivers can be loving and ever-present yet raise a child with low self-esteem because he or she has certain personality traits. Another youngster could be raised in the most difficult circumstances imaginable and emerge as a strong leader and successful person due to their inborn strengths. Across this spectrum, all children form *I am* beliefs within the environments in which they are raised.

Due to their cause-and-effect thinking, kids turn environments, the treatment they receive, and the words they hear in combination with innate personalities, into conscious or unconscious *I am* beliefs. Bad situations make kids feel badly, from which they can form the belief *I am bad*. Positive responses toward kids can lead to the internal belief *I am good*. Due to a young person's natural strengths and weaknesses, such beliefs can externalize as

30

people-pleasing, performance-orientation or appropriate levels of high self-esteem. Without adults knowing it, youngsters are at risk for using everything that happens to and around them in the formation of their self-identities, including circumstances which have nothing to do with their worth.

I AM BELIEFS - POSITIVE
Relationships

Important adults caring for a child in a genuine, supportive relationship is the first and foremost contributor to a child's positive *I am* belief. The most helpful environment is one in which adults meet the young person's needs and appropriately attune to the youngster's signals for food, sleep, stimulation and closeness. This attunement instills a sense that kids are important, loved and deserved to be well cared for. From an infant's perspective, the world is complete when important others attach to them and make it safe for the infant to be dependent in return. In spite of human limitations, and the fact that no child will have a perfect childhood environment, adults moving toward youngsters in genuine, caring relationships is the primary way that kids come to believe *I matter, I am valuable,* and *I deserve love and attention.* It is hard for young people to draw these conclusions about themselves without supportive relationships initiated and sustained by adults.

Relationships matter in every phase of life. Infants need care and attachment, young children need soothing and discipline, and all young people benefit from peer friendships and the support of older adults, such as grandparents, mentors and teachers. Even the most introverted child needs to perceive they matter to important others. Youngsters may be quite introverted and spend many hours in activities by themselves, but the relational environment that sends the message *You are being supported by others and it is safe to be yourself here* is usually interpreted by kids as positive *I am* beliefs. Intimacy is the sharing of true selves between people. Safe, genuine intimacy—with or without words—creates positive *I am* beliefs. Intimacy is only created in relationships. Every relationship in life has the potential to send *I am* information to young people.

Attunement

The safety and value of relationships is taken to new levels when the qualities of attunement are present. Attunement is the capacity to read verbal and nonverbal signals of another person and respond with appropriate care. Parents who read the signals of their children and respond with supportive, soothing actions are well-attuned caregivers. Settling a fussy infant, kindly responding to a toddler who is hurt and listening to teens in a way that works for them are examples of attunement.

The most satisfying relationships are ones in which attunement is a central component, which is true for infants through adults. An attuned response from another heightens the sense of self gained from relationships because attunement is a positive, reflective mirror. It implies the receiver of attunement is worth the time and sensitivity for having their needs met. As young people receive the messages of being worth an adult's time through positive attunement, the likelihood increases that kids will form positive *I am* beliefs.

It's okay to not be okay

One of the most powerful, attuned messages a childhood environment can communicate to a youngster is *it's okay to not be okay*, meaning it's safe to be yourself and make mistakes. Environments where young people are supported and accepted—even when they do not meet the expectations or guidelines of that environment —are places where kids develop positive *I am* beliefs. I am not describing permissive parenting without guidelines and expectations for appropriate behavior. Instead, I am advocating for parenting in which behavioral guidelines are clear and wrong-doing does not turn into shaming and belittling for kids. In order to thrive in the intimacy of important relationships, young people must feel safe enough to make mistakes, including big mistakes, and not be disqualified from ongoing connection to their important communities, including their families. Believing *I'm so bad I don't deserve friends or support* can be a precursor to addiction, or other numbing and dissociating behaviors. In order to form positive *I am* beliefs, kids need to know *it's okay to not be okay.*

Telling a young person *it's okay to not be okay* reinforces the message that it's alright to make mistakes. Parents may understand that all youngsters make mistakes, but young people don't arrive at the same conclusion if cultural or family settings require something different from them. People of all ages create punishments for themselves when they fail to meet their own or others' expectations. An environment where perfection is not the goal, and social belonging continues in spite of wrongdoing, reassures kids that life is not singularly based on performance and success. Telling youngsters *it's okay to not be okay* and reinforcing the message with attuned connection when things go wrong, increases the probability that kids will be accepting of themselves and others when inevitable disappointments arise.

Positive Statements

Supportive, truthful words help young people form positive *I am* beliefs. Many adults have relayed examples of a parent or important other who spoke truth into their lives which they could not have discerned on their own at their age and maturity level. Childhood seems like a level playing field to kids—their peer group is comprised of kindergarteners, third graders or high schoolers just like themselves, and virtually all young people want to be successful and well-liked by their peers. Young people use this peer environment as a feedback loop. Resulting levels of success in these social and academic arenas form into *I am* beliefs that may or may not be accurate. Therefore, youngsters benefit from having adults speak positive words into their lives beyond school environments.

For example, one client, a sixteen-year-old, struggled with reading and writing throughout high school. His teachers recommended professional testing for learning disabilities. After a thorough evaluation, it was apparent no obvious learning disabilities stood in the way of the teenager's academic success. The professional who evaluated him said to the young man, "You have the intellectual capacity to earn a Ph.D if you want to." The student had high ability and low performance. The professional spoke to his capability to be successful in the very arena where he was struggling.

When I met the man as a graduate student, he said, "I wasn't interested in what they were asking me to read or write in high school,

33

but I never forgot what the psychologist said to me about my ability." Today he is succeeding in a strenuous graduate program because he is interested in the material and invested in the outcome of his work. During his teen years, his peer environment might have implied the young man was a failure, but the words of an adult impacted his experience with life-changing truth.

Other influential words spoken to youngsters include a mother who said to her teenage daughter who was struggling academically, "You are very kind and your ability to make friends is one of your strengths. I know you will be successful in life."

The teenager could not quite believe her mother's words, but I validated that her mother was right. I added, "Emotional intelligence is a better predictor of success than academic achievement and you have high emotional intelligence. I'm sure you will be successful in life like your mother said."

Truthful, positive words spoken to young people help them form positive *I am* beliefs when they cannot see their own innate capabilities. As mentioned, life mirrors a sense of self back to kids, and adults are a major component of that reflection. Choosing to speak positive, truthful words about many aspects of kids' lives, including qualities and capabilities they would not otherwise discern on their own, plants positive *I am* seeds which can bear fruit for a lifetime.

I AM BELIEFS - NEGATIVE
Disappointment and Perceived Inferiority

Negative *I am* beliefs may be the easiest to develop. When life does not give children positive responses for an unlimited number of reasons, it is easy to turn those circumstances into negative *I am* beliefs. When kids do their best and life does not turn out as hoped, or they compare themselves to peers and find themselves inferior in some way, they wonder *What's wrong with me? Why can't I be like other kids?* Perceived defeats can translate into self-perception that there is something wrong with the child. Caregivers generally do not know kids are heading into this emotional terrain when they fail or express their disappointment. Not all losses and regrets mean youngsters will see themselves in a negative light, but adults are generally not aware how ordinary losses, personal mistakes, and comments from others morph into negative *I am* beliefs in young people's minds. Kids come up with negative *I am* beliefs when they look in the mirror of life and the reflection they see tells them they have failed to meet their own or someone else's expectations.

For example, a college student described a situation where she was assigned a science project at eight years old. The third-grader recruited her parents' help and together they spent many hours working on the project per the child's understanding of the directions. When the science fair projects were turned in and displayed for students and parents to view, it was clear the young student had misunderstood the directions. She completely failed the project and was devastated. The worst impact of the science fair mishap was her perception that her parents had failed her. She began to believe she could not trust her parents—they were no longer a reliable support system for her. The student lived the remainder of her years at home in fear she might misunderstand something else and she was conflicted about whether her parents could be trusted. The adults in her life had no idea her internal world had been upended by the science fair outcome and that her sense of self was significantly shaped by the failure.

In a counseling session, the client's third-grade-self came to understand she had personally misunderstood the directions and her parents had followed her lead. The child's loss and misperceived failure were resolved. The timing for the session was important because the young woman was on the verge of moving to another community to start her first professional position. Her greatest insecurity was that she would not understand what was expected of her in the new job and others would fail to support her —both of which came from earlier beliefs. Her identity had been incorrectly formed by disappointment and perceived inferiority in her childhood. These fears carried into her future with erroneous *I am* beliefs.

Negative Environments and Mistreatment

Many adults do not know kids transfer their negative environments and mistreatment into negative beliefs about themselves. Poverty, chronically unemployed parents, alcoholism, drug addiction, neglect, violence, verbal abuse and sexual abuse can all seep into the mindsets of young people as personal failure. Is it misguided for kids to take personally something over which they have no control? Yes. Yet many children think their caregiver's behavior, circumstances and mistreatment of them is due to the young person's lack of value. Teachers face this challenge in education when a student's low sense of self, influenced by the conditions in which they live, hinder them from seeing themselves and their academic potential accurately. All kids are innately lovable and important. A young person's innate value is not tied to their surroundings yet not all kids intrinsically know they are important, valuable and lovable—especially when their conditions and adult caregivers model something different. Negative modeling, mistreatment and poor living conditions often load into the minds of young people as something inherently wrong about themselves.

Another liability for children raised in circumstances with violence, addiction and abuse is that adults with these lifestyles generally have their own low self-esteem. Since kids learn through modeling, and adults transfer what is inside them to their offspring, the dysfunction and abuse children are exposed to in their environments can unconsciously become their programming.

In my experience, young people who understand themselves beyond their environments are a minority. Some kids naturally think *I don't want my life to be like the one I'm living* and set their sights for a different lifestyle for adulthood. Yet many youngsters interpret their caregivers' lifestyles, and the treatment they receive, as something about themselves. They use these conditions to form *I am* beliefs. They think *If my life is bad, there must be something wrong with me—I am bad.*

Emotional Reactions of Others

Positive and negative *I am* beliefs are also derived from the reactions of others. Kids are constantly reading the adults in their environments for clues to their own identity. A positive reaction from an adult in a young person's life can mean *I am good* and a negative reaction from someone can mean *I am bad.* Generally, young people lack the maturity and sophistication to apply complex thinking to understand someone else's emotional world. For example, a teacher who is upset by difficult circumstances in their private life might be unusually impatient with students. In such a case, some students will erroneously ascribe the teacher's impatience to their own performance and feel badly about themselves as a result.

A child's sensitivity and attachment to an important adult influences the impact an adult's emotional reaction has on the young person's *I am* belief. A parent's words and emotional response can have more impact than almost any other force in a youngster's life, as evidenced by the following story.

A man told me he was the salutatorian of his high school graduating class, which meant he had the second highest grade point average in a class of 600 students. Yet his father was quite disappointed. Because he was not the valedictorian—the student with the highest grade point average—the young man failed to please his father. The father demeaned the student's success and responded with irritability and negative judgment. The client interpreted his father's response to mean he fell short of the mark as a student, as a son, and in many ways, as a person. His 'failure' —as it was reflected by his father's reaction—became part of the student's self-identity. The man sought counseling because he was depressed. His negative *I am* belief factored into his depression even though according to most standards he was a very talented and successful individual.

Negative *I am* beliefs are derived from critical words spoken by others, personal traits such as appearance which are considered inferior, lack of respect, being disregarded and being used by others. Physical violence and sexual abuse in all forms generally communicates to youngsters that they are not valuable and lovable. Almost any experience children perceive in a negative light—whether or not it is perceived as negative by adults—can lead to erroneous negative *I am* beliefs, unless these experiences are understood correctly, and processed with adults who view the situation from the child's lens and speak truth into it.

Choices for the Child's Benefit

It is not uncommon for kids to internalize a negative sense of self from actions that are taken to protect and support them. Children who are adopted as infants usually have some form of negative *I am* beliefs in their hearts, derived from their young thinking. They perceive themselves as different from other kids and often their differences are interpreted as something bad about themselves, rather than as a circumstance about their birth parents. In many cases, it is possible to explain to kids the reasons they were adopted when they are old enough to understand, but these truths do not always change the way young people perceive themselves. The young, confused infants who lose their bearings after adoption do not have intellectual understanding of what happened to them, and this confusion is retained internally. Commonly, this confusion and heartache contribute to a degree of negative self-identity.

Kids who need special education, remedial intervention of any kind, or have medical conditions can be particularly vulnerable to seeing themselves in a negative light. Young people want to be normal. Normal means being like other kids and having what other kids have. Deviations from the norm—even when they are interventions put in place for the young person's benefit—can be negatively interpreted by kids and turned into negative *I am* beliefs.

When I am counseling clients, I work to understand the views they hold about themselves within the problems they are describing. Often an erroneous view of self is one of the most painful aspects of what troubles kids of all ages. A negative *I am* belief is virtually always lurking in the problems clients present, whether they are describing trauma, difficulties in school, relationships, or the normal challenges of life.

A negative *I am* belief is like the tiny bit of debris which gathers dust, dirt and sticky crumbs around it until it is a hardened clump. As the years pass, more accurate or inaccurate interpretations of life pile onto the original cluster. Eventually, the client has an established mental program pertaining to the negative *I am* belief. As clients unfold the layers of the problem which brought them to counseling, we peel away the metaphoric debris and other matter that has collected on the original, inaccurate sense of self. It is always there. Negative *I am* beliefs are part of why clients are stuck.

All young people possess inherent skills and abilities; sadly, negative *I am* beliefs can mislead them into not seeing their innate value. Children of all ages can see themselves in very limited and inaccurate ways when they have been neglected, mistreated, or given messages which contribute to a negative sense of self.

Viewpoint Matters

The power of the internal belief is being validated by quantum physics. Light can be measured as a wave or as particles. How light appears when being measured is determined by the tools scientists choose for measuring it. If the observer sets up equipment to measure light as a wave, light appears as a wave. The same is true if the observer sets up equipment to measure light as particles —light appears in the investigator's lens as particles. The living nature of light responds to the observer's choice.

This scientific understanding suggests that life shows up for people in part based on how they view it. What lenses are kids using to view their worlds? They are using the lenses of self-identity. What they get back from life is influenced, in part, by how they see the world from their viewpoints. The perspective used to view life shapes one's satisfaction and fulfillment. Self-identity results. For these reasons, it is important to consider the *I am* beliefs young people are internalizing during their growing up years.

By adulthood, many individuals have determined who they are by their experiences and find their perspectives confirmed— not because the viewpoint is true in later life, but because they are using a pre-determined perspective. Felicity's story is an example of how people read life circumstances from an interior lens, which may or may not correspond with the actual facts.

Felicity is a 13-year-old girl who told me in counseling that she did not have very many friends at school. I inquired further and learned she was regularly invited to birthday parties and played on the school's soccer team. I asked what she did during lunch time, suspecting it would be a good indicator of her actual friendship circle.

"I either sit with the soccer girls or I go to different tables and talk to people," she answered.

"Friends?" I asked.

"Well, sort of," she answered. "Not close friends, but I don't want to be locked into any one social group."

As I learned more about her social experience in middle school, it appeared Felicity was liked well enough, but was insecure like many young adolescents. She described her internal sense of self and said, "I'm not as pretty and thin as the other girls in my school. I'm not as good as other kids."

I viewed the young student to be lovely, but I knew my perception would not shift Felicity's internal view of herself. She believed *I am not pretty like other girls; I am not as well-liked as others;* and *I'm not smart or successful like some kids."*

I asked about her grades.

Felicity said, "I get pretty good grades, but not like my older brother."

She also told me she was elected to student government, which I presumed meant she was regarded well enough by her peers to be chosen by them.

Felicity had a view of herself on the inside that did not match what appeared to be true about her from the outside. Her *I am* beliefs, which in part appeared to be erroneous, carried much more weight for determining her happiness than what was actually true. It is normal for teenagers to be insecure about their appearance and compare themselves to peers, but there are life-long consequences for kids who are misguided by inaccurate, internal *I am* beliefs throughout their lives. As Felicity's example conveys, an internally held belief can carry more weight in shaping a person's reality than the truth.

Summary

A person can be a genius and think *I am dumb* because others, life experiences, or internal judgments cause them to think incorrectly about themselves. People choose their vocations, partners and overall life experiences based on how they view themselves. Circumstances can keep individuals from fulfilling their potential, but often, the true inhibitors to a meaningful and fulfilling life are based within and correlated to *I am* beliefs.

I am beliefs matter because they are the internal road maps, which direct an individual's choices. When youngsters come to decision-making points large and small, unconscious *I am* beliefs weigh greatly in their decisions. *Am I deserving or not? Am I good enough to try or should I exclude myself before I begin? Am I a winner or a loser?* The realistic answer to these questions is not as important as the self-perceived answers to these questions.

Toddlers through twenty-five-year-olds use life as a learning laboratory to derive *I am* beliefs about themselves. *I am* beliefs include: *I am smart, funny, handsome, weak, worthwhile, lovable, unlovable, better than other kids, less than other kids, a bully, a winner, a loser, too fat, too skinny, too noisy, too lonely, too boisterous, too boring, too smart, too dumb, too active, too dull, insignificant, inadequate, incompetent, a failure*, etc.

In summary, people are prone to convert life experiences into unconscious *I am* beliefs. Life's joys, challenges, and interactions seep into the conscious and unconscious minds of kids as personal concepts about themselves. Eventually, repeated ideas like *I am* beliefs turn into internal programs that run on their own. Once *I am* concepts are established in the mind, a person will often respond to life as if it matched the internal negative view—even when external conditions may be better than their *I am* beliefs suggest.

PRINCIPLE FOUR—*CHILDREN DEVELOP STRATEGIES IN RESPONSE TO THEIR SITUATIONS. THEIR STRATEGIES CONTINUE INTO THE FUTURE.*

Strategies are the coping mechanisms people develop to adjust to their circumstances. They are the emotional and behavioral responses young people use to fit in, calm down, be successful, seek attention, avoid attention, perform well, avoid problems or any other adaptive response to life. Because their minds are in the process of development, youngsters use unconscious, immature perspectives to interpret events and adjust their behavior to what is happening around them. Essentially, they use young understanding to interpret the world and behave accordingly. If kids have negative experiences, they develop strategies to prevent negative experiences from reoccurring or to help them cope. Positive experiences prompt youngsters to develop responses that increase the likelihood positive experiences will reoccur. Some strategies are successful and represent high emotional intelligence. Other strategies are immature, and sometimes self-injurious, but are a young person's best attempt to survive.

Strategies reflect a person's inherent personality. They are derived directly from a person's lived experience as well as their natural personality traits. An extroverted leader will respond to problems by using leadership skills and attempting to enlist others to help. An introverted person may be inclined to quietly solve a problem alone. A naturally funny person will use humor to distract from pain or break into hilarity when things get difficult whether or not humor is appropriate to the circumstance. The adaptive measures to life's situations reflect an individual's temperament, skills and culture.

One family's situation provides an illustration of strategy development. Their fifteen-year-old son worked at a nearby grocery store. When the family relocated to another home in the area they asked their son to bring home boxes for packing. He began bringing home two to five boxes a day, which they greatly appreciated. Their genuine response was a form of positive conditioning which rewarded him for what he contributed to the family. Rewarded behavior is generally repeated.

For the sake of this example, imagine the difficulty which would have followed if the son who had been positively rewarded for bringing boxes home when they were needed, continued to bring home two to five boxes a day for the rest of the months he worked at the grocery store. As the boxes piled up, the family would have become frustrated with their son's behavior. This example speaks to the nature of strategies: 1) They start for a good a reason, and 2) A once useful strategy can become a problem rather than a solution if continued beyond the initial need.

Many of the problems, which lead caregivers to take their children for counseling, are due to the strategies young people developed earlier in life. Because strategies, which were used to counteract the circumstances at one time of life continue unconsciously later, some coping strategies become more problematic than the original circumstance that preceded them. For example, children who do not have enough food may develop a pattern of food hoarding. Once they are no longer in dire conditions, kids may continue to hoard food because the mind and body continue to run the food hoarding program. It is not uncommon for foster parents who provide plenty of nutrition to find youngsters hiding food after they have lived in deprivation. More than one family has brought their children to counseling due to the food hoarding that follows a young person's adoption out of neglect and deprivation.

It is not uncommon for children, including very young children, to develop the habit of masturbating for self-soothing. Unfortunately, youngsters who rely on this strategy cannot help but use it in most situations which distress them, including day care, school and other settings. Eventually the problem that brings them to counseling is their masturbation in public settings, directly motivated by their distress, which they could not find any other way to manage. Without an adult to comfort and connect with kids when they were frightened, alone, or upset, kids find their own methods for self-soothing, and these methods operate reflexively as needed. They become programmed strategies the body-brain uses automatically like the capacity to read.

Kids often get in trouble for the methods they use for self-soothing. Strategies like food hoarding and masturbating in the classroom need to be curtailed yet they speak to a difficulty underneath the strategy. Simply punishing young people for problematic behavior may be over-emphasizing the strategy and missing the distress behind the problem. It is useful to consider the source behind the strategy, and address both as needed. People adapt to their circumstances. Kids want to find equilibrium in their lives and sometimes their best methods, although temporarily effective, may eventually create other problems in their lives.

An adult told me about a repetitive childhood dream which displayed her adaptive strategy. She often dreamt that she and her little dog Tippy were holding up the back of the family station wagon to keep it from going over a cliff. Her family was not doing well at the time and as a frightened, immature child she believed *I am responsible for keeping my family from going over the edge.* Did this person actually have the power to resolve her family's problems? No, but her environment suggested she should do something to keep her world in balance. As the dream suggests, she developed a detrimental and long-lasting strategy to be responsible for more than she could handle as a quasi-adult in her family. Not surprisingly, her childhood strategy continued into adulthood where she is overly responsible with family members, including her grandchildren.

Dissociation

As briefly mentionezd previously, dissociation is often a young person's first defensive strategy. Dissociation is an attempt to remove one's self emotionally from a situation where the body has to be present. In some cases, it is the only strategy available to young people and they become masters at it. The more bad things that happen to kids, the more capable they become at separating themselves emotionally from what they are experiencing. Neglect and abuse generally lead to dissociation, which like other strategies, become problems well after the original situations are over.

Not being able to remember childhood is an example of dissociation. Young people who can't remember much about their younger years where memory is normally present, generally had to use the strategy of dissociation to manage what was happening to and around them. They can't remember something well because they were trying to avoid experiencing it – in other words, they were trying not to give it their attention. The brain uses the degree of attention as one of the signals to determine what is important to store in concrete memory and what can be sloughed off. In counseling, one of the first problems to solve may be the young client's dissociation, which was a vital coping tool during difficult times, but has become the problem that motivates a family to seek professional help. The discussion about coping strategies would not be well represented without this invisible method kids use to try to make themselves feel okay.

As mentioned, coping strategies do not always come with an off switch. Once adaptive strategies are in place, they are ready to assert themselves when conditions trigger them. Sometimes strategies are appropriate to the moment, but they are not always effective for a lifetime. For example, children who are reinforced for being helpless in childhood, will find themselves naturally using the same strategy throughout life. Helplessness is not an overly attractive or effective trait for success. An overly responsible youngster who adapted to difficult circumstances by parenting younger children, will continue to operate with a caretaking role for many years to come. People often come to counseling because a strategy that was helpful at one point has become the problem that motivates them to get help.

Strategy development is a learned process, and like other learning, it forms into neural networks held within the body-mind to operate unconsciously. Unconscious material is very useful because pre-loaded neural networks allow us to read, drive, and brush our teeth without re-learning these skills every day. Yet sometimes automatic strategies are a mismatch to ever-changing life circumstances. As the grocery worker's story illustrates, it is not always useful for strategies developed at one point in life to continue for the remainder of life.

With consciousness, caring and intentionality, adults can intercept the strategies they see young people developing. The first step is to bring truth to the child's heart and mind about the situation and to give them accurate, appropriate information to help them revise their coping strategies.

Giving appropriate information to youngsters is useful and caregivers need to be mindful of their motives as they help young people interpret their situations. For example, giving a child difficult information about a parent can be handled in various ways, each of which will create different responses and different strategies for the child. Telling young people that a parent is going to drug treatment can be done so it is supportive to the children's natural love and protection of the parent, or it can communicate condemnation of the drug-using parent and fear for the youngster. Reassuring kids that they did nothing wrong to cause the problem—but Mom or Dad needs a doctor to help them get well—creates a compassionate environment in which kids can develop healthier coping strategies. In contrast, telling young people their mother or father is a drug addict and always will be, creates a different emotional response. This scenario generates the need for defensive strategies from a young person who could easily interpret the situation to mean *I am not as good as other kids because my parent is a drug addict.* Kids incorporate their parents' problems into their own identities unless intercepted. The scenario of a parent seeking treatment can be presented in different ways, which creates various self-judgments and strategy development in kids. Knowing young people develop coping mechanisms to deal with life circumstances can help caregivers address this aspect of their young lives.

Humans develop behavioral responses to life because they are adaptive learners. Repeated responses become patterns, and patterns eventually become automatic strategies. It is often young people's adaptive strategies that lead families into counseling. Therefore, it is wise to understand the messages young people perceive, identify their strategies, and give them accurate, helpful information to counteract negative coping methods. In short, kids need help from grownups in order to cope with life in appropriate ways.

Andrea's story summarizes the four principles mentioned in this chapter. Andrea was a medical doctor who struggled in her professional life. She became the victim of sexual abuse beginning at age three and each of the four principles of young people's thinking is evident in her story:

1. Children perceive the world with themselves at the center; they use personal, cause-and-effect thinking to understand their worlds.

Andrea believed she caused the sexual abuse to occur. Her concrete, cause-and-effect thinking led her to surmise with a young mind that in some way she was responsible for the perpetrator's unwanted behavior.

2. Children take words at face value; they believe what they are told.

Andrea's perpetrator spoke about Andrea's specialness and offered her gifts and favors. His words, and the favoritism he showed, meant Andrea was important and loved. Feeling badly, while also being told she was special, created confusion for Andrea, and the perpetrator's words overrode her own sense of what was happening to her.

46

3. Children are prone to form *I am* beliefs; their *I am* beliefs influence their future.

Andrea's *I am* beliefs included *I am a bad girl* and *I don't deserve better love.* She interpreted the ongoing difficult situation with its bad feelings to mean there was something wrong with her, therefore she was unworthy of safe love.

4. Children develop strategies in response to their situations; their strategies become life-long patterns.

Andrea reflected a degree of narcissism about her intelligence and "specialness" to her peers, which alienated her from her community, and her negative self-views led to detrimental choices. Andrea treated herself like she was treated in her childhood situation: very special and quite dissociated. Andrea's dissociation later in life impaired her. She was cited for inattentiveness in her work, which was actually her body's long-lasting strategy of dissociation.

As we worked through the healing process, Andrea said with shock, "I have never once in my life believed anything other than what I believed at age three! I still assume I caused the abuse to happen and therefore I am very bad." Even though she is a successful doctor, Andrea held within her body a child's perspective derived from her experiences at three years old.

I helped her insert truth where a very negative sense of self had settled, unfiltered, into her body. Not surprisingly, Andrea believed she caused a current bad work circumstance to happen, which she did not cause, and that there was something very wrong with her. Andrea's most problematic strategy carried from childhood was her tendency to dissociate and become emotionally frozen when triggers from her childhood trauma were activated by her stressful work environment. Because the childhood strategies activated in her adult body, Andrea was at a loss for appropriate, situational responses. She experienced parts of her adult life with the same template established during her childhood, even though she was an intelligent, capable adult.

As Andrea's story portrays, the thoughts, misperceptions, concreteness and strategies of childhood become operating systems for the future.

SUMMARY

An old-fashioned saying purports the world is our oyster, implying that our individual lives—the pearls—emerge from the grit and grind of everyday life. If the world is our oyster, it is an oyster-shaped learning lab in which the words, feelings, actions, nuances, experiences, or absence of these in our lives is used to make meaning about ourselves, others and the world at large. Young people often interact with this feedback loop from the vantage point of themselves at the center. Due to their simplistic, cause-and-effect thinking, it is not uncommon for kids to assume they are responsible for what happens around them.

Young people also take words at face value, which many adults do not fully realize. Children of all ages misperceive teasing and take negative comments as real even if they were meant to be playful. Toddlers through late twenty-somethings believe what is said to them, often literally, and seldom ask for confirmation or understanding about what they hear.

Humans develop a *sensing-self*—a way to read people, environments, and their own interactions with the world. On many levels, the sensing-self translates life experiences into a form of thinking and believing which becomes cellular memory. Many of the ideas held within the mind and body reflect *I am* beliefs that became established in childhood and play out for the remainder of life. These cellular memories activate on their own, independent from conscious thinking, and are influential after the initial information was stored.

Finally, individuals find ways to cope with their experiences in life. Many of these coping mechanisms develop in childhood and form into long-lasting strategies. These strategies endure not because people wish to act like kids in adult circumstances, but because the mind and body run their adaptive programs until they are intercepted and healed.

These are the reasons it is important to find out what young people are thinking and what beliefs they are beginning to hold. A direct way to find out what kids think is to ask them. They usually respond with authenticity when asked questions such as,

"Did you think this..." or "What do you think was meant by...?" Straightforward questions will often yield straightforward answers. The following chapter presents ways to help kids according to the four principles mentioned in this chapter.

Chapter Three
What to Do About What Children Believe

Sometimes kids perceive the world correctly and come to insightful, accurate understanding about themselves and their situations. I am always impressed when I run across young people who can do this. I respond with something like, "Wow, how did you figure that out?"

They answer, "I don't know, I just did," or "I knew it wasn't about me so why should I worry about it?" I'm glad there are young people in the world who naturally understand situations correctly.

More often though, due to the four points previously discussed —*I caused it, I believe it, I am...because of it, and I adapt to it*—kids of all ages misperceive situations to be about themselves and follow with responses that might be helpful in the short run, but are not good, long-lasting ways to approach problems. It is wise for caregivers to help kids understand situations correctly and to give them appropriate truth whenever possible. With attunement to the individual person, the following steps usually bring some degree of understanding and relief to young people. These three responses can give young children through twenty-somethings the ability to move forward knowing which part of a situation is about them, and which part is someone else's responsibility. The three steps are:

1) Clarify how young people understand situations and help them identify related thoughts, feelings and *I am*

statements. As discussed, it can be quite surprising how young people interpret circumstances.

2) Validate them with pertinent, accurate reflections using phrases such as, "Most people would feel the same way if this happened to them." Validation is usually followed by observable relief and a request for more confirmation.

3) Clarify the truth and who has the power. Truth appropriately shared can be life-changing. The truth about power can be powerful.

The entry to this three-step process requires a version of *Tell me what you're thinking*...so the adult listener can comprehend what a young person is saying and doing. The goal is for an adult to understand how a young person's thinking makes sense to them, validating with phrases like, "I can see how that makes sense from your perspective." Further conversation can help identify where the power lies for best solutions. Each of these steps is developed more fully in the following pages.

1. *CLARIFY HOW A YOUNG PERSON UNDERSTANDS*

As mentioned, young people use positive and negative experiences to form their self-identities. Sometimes they make accurate assessments in their circumstances, but other times they come to erroneous conclusions about themselves and others. Unfortunately, they develop ineffective long-term strategies as a result of what they have experienced or believed. One of the first steps to understand kids' behavior is to clarify what young people are thinking and feeling about the words, behavior and circumstances around them, which is a powerful entry point into helping shape their beliefs. Clarifying is the initial tool for launching interventions that can keep young people moving forward in life with truth and support.

Clarification should take place in an appropriate moment without putting kids into an emotional double-bind if they answer honestly. An example of a double-bind question is asking an adolescent who is being teased, "You know we're just kidding, don't you?" Peer pressure in most cases would mean the teen could only give one response—a cavalier, "Yeah." No matter how the teenager actually felt, they would be unlikely to answer with a true report of thoughts and feelings about being teased.

The type of clarification I am recommending takes place in a safe environment and provides the opportunity for kids to respond honestly. It involves 1) discovering how children think and feel in their situations, and 2) checking to see how they understand a problem to be about themselves. Adults can ask clear, direct questions when young people feel safe enough to answer honestly. The purpose of this intervention is to understand how kids have interpreted the words, behaviors and circumstances around them as well as to give them correct information pertaining to the situation. It can be done naturally and playfully. With very young children in my office I grab a stuffed animal and say to the plush toy, "Did you feel bad when...?" and I fill in the blank with the circumstance that happened to the child. I look at the youngster for the answer, who usually nods with their own feelings and thoughts. I can continue interacting with the plush toy and receiving information from the young client until I understand how the child perceived a situation and what they are believing about themselves as a result.

Teenagers can be asked directly. Clarifying what is happening in the minds and hearts of kids big and small is very empowering to them. It is so effective it can be used in place of discipline in some cases. Because everyone's thinking makes sense to them, understanding the context, interpretation and meaning derived from young people's interactions in life can be a guide into shaping their behavior. One example comes from an elementary school in Spokane, WA, which found the yearly suspension rate for students decrease from 129 suspensions per year to 48 total suspensions over a four-year period. The dramatic decrease occurred when staff began talking to students about the emotional and situational aspects of their lives outside of school. Rather than immediately suspend students as punishment for misbehavior, administrators sought to understand the circumstances surrounding their problematic behavior. Understanding what was happening away from school directly influenced how often youngsters attended school. Helping kids process their challenges, including those away from school, enabled them be more resilient in the social and academic settings of their classrooms.

Thinking and Feeling

Making sense of the ways people understand their worlds includes differentiating feeling and thinking—two sides of the same coin. Many people believe feelings stand alone, yet thoughts influence feelings. Cognition precedes emotion. Because thinking and feeling are intricately intertwined, it is important to identify how youngsters think in a situation as well as their feelings about it. Winning the lottery or going bankrupt produce different emotional responses depending on how someone thinks about the implications of each scenario. A young child would not feel excitement about winning the lottery unless the child had a certain understanding of money, nor would a young person be emotionally impacted by bankruptcy unless the child had accurate thoughts about bankruptcy's implications.

Another example of thoughts preceding emotion is the scenario of a driver stopped on railroad tracks waiting for a traffic light. If the driver thinks a train might come and hit the car, the driver will feel anxious whether or not a train is coming down the tracks. If the driver thinks they are waiting on an abandoned line where it is not possible for a train to be on the tracks, the driver will feel at ease even if a locomotive is just around the corner.

The internal world of thinking and feeling is complex and much of it occurs unconsciously. Thinking often happens automatically without conscious choice, and people often react emotionally without knowing what they are thinking. Feelings emerge which cannot clearly be identified until people have searched inside to find the cause for joy or distress.

Tom Hilton, a colleague and friend, identified a common pattern for emotions he termed *The Shame Barrel*. Anger is first, followed by hurt, fear, self-pity, and shame. All five feelings are present in every painful situation. Hilton trained me to look for these five emotional states within my clients. By identifying these basic feelings and naming the circumstances or perspectives which led to them, clients can usually begin to dissipate the energy of their emotions.

Hilton's exercise is very simple and can be coached by leading the upset person through these statements:

> *I feel mad because...*
> *I feel hurt because...*
> *I feel fear because...*
> *I feel self-pity because...*
> *I feel shame because ....*

Each statement is followed with a *brief* (one sentence or phrase) description of the circumstance and thinking, which led to the specific feeling. The listener is required to hear the statements without defensiveness or arguing. If needed, the parties can each use the shame barrel as a beginning point to decrease emotionality and start a constructive conversation without over-reaction. Hilton states, "Every person is entitled to their own feelings."

When parents, kids, and friends use the shame barrel, emotion is dissipated, people understand how the other person's thinking makes sense to them, and emotional intimacy is usually achieved. Without expression of feelings and their sources, people seek ways to defend themselves and overreact to situations. Many of the choices that follow unexpressed ideas and feelings—such as being enraged, hurting others, hurting one's self, and making poor life choices—are a direct result of not knowing what is happening emotionally on the inside and overreacting to life, which can be counter to an individual's best interests.

Hilton's last feeling in the shame barrel deserves special attention because it is one of the most painful emotions to experience. Shame can be so hard to tolerate that people develop automatic defenses so they do not have to consciously know they are feeling shame. The strong emotion of shame is diverted away from consciousness because it implies a deficiency of self—not just a sense of wrong doing, but an overarching sense of wrong-being, which is personal identity. The feeling of shame equates to, *I am so bad I am ineligible to be in my community.*

Shame leads people to hide, withdraw from their relationships and medicate with drugs, alcohol and other means. When addictive types of behavior are repeated, shame is generally underneath the behavior, even if it is unconscious.

Due to the painful nature of shame, kids will probably not offer it when asked the simple question, "How do you feel?" The feelings of happiness, anger, sadness and fear are usually identified more readily than the deeper, more complex emotions like betrayal, jealousy and shame. If we ask young people only the straightforward question, "How do you feel?" they will give us straightforward answers which will only represent their first layer of feelings. Beneath the first layer of feelings are deeper emotions which are important to identify because they drive unconscious behavior. Emotions such as shame are powerful forces that move people into intense and sometimes irrational behavior they cannot prevent or explain. Hilton's shame barrel is one way to access and understand the feelings along with the thinking behind young people's actions.

As a further illustration, the power of the thinking-feeling-behavior combination can be found in the case of a ninth grader who is the only player to make the varsity soccer team. He might feel insecure, yet also be very proud. The soccer player might think *I am a great soccer player* until he begins to practice with the varsity squad and discovers he is not as strong, fast, or developed as some of the other players. In the case of boys, it is very possible that a freshman player would not be as big as an 18-year-old senior in high school. The ninth grader might be given very little playing time and very little inclusion in the social aspects of varsity soccer. Then the young player might think *I'm inferior. I'm bad at soccer. No one likes me. I'm a failure.* In summary, making the varsity team can generate positive thoughts and feelings at one point; not playing in varsity games or being excluded may generate negative thoughts and feelings. How the player responds in the various situations is greatly influenced by how the player thinks about himself and the situation. Clarifying thoughts and feelings is the pathway into helping young people cope.

If the young soccer player can accurately identify his feelings, he is likely to have the best response in the circumstance. At practice, the ninth grader might be aware of his insecurities and be less skilled than older players, but if he thinks, *I've been given a great opportunity to learn and develop so I'll do the best I can,* the young player will increase the likelihood of being accepted and will grow as a young athlete.

If the ninth grader thinks *I got selected for the varsity team and I deserve more playing time,* the student may act in an entitled way and generate a different reaction from the other varsity players. In many cases, adolescent peers who find a teammate inappropriately elevating themselves will create the opportunity to 'put that player in their place.' Shame and distress usually follow.

Perhaps the young player interprets his insecurities as *I never should have made the varsity soccer team. The coach is only using me to fill out the roster, but the coach doesn't really care about me.* In this case, the young player may give off an air that says, *I don't really belong here and I know you don't like me anyway,* which could lead to different interactions with teammates. What follows could be less inclusion and a less satisfying year as a freshman on the varsity soccer team.

Several ways of thinking and feeling are represented in each of the above scenarios. The three very different ways of thinking lead into different ways of responding to the situation. The ninth grader's thoughts and feelings have the potential to create different responses from others as well.

Another example of the thinking-feeling-behaving combination is evident in young children who face circumstances like being removed from unsafe households and placed into foster care. Most kids, no matter their age, will attribute such trauma as something bad about themselves. Unless an adult takes time to understand how a child is thinking and explain a situation correctly, kids can blame themselves for being removed from the people they love. Young people do not like being in painful conditions yet they generally feel love and loyalty to their parents and want to stay with them. Michael Oher's story in Chapter One is an example of a child's love and loyalty to his mother and many siblings.

Everyone's Thinking Makes Sense to Them

People do what they do for a reason—even when those around them cannot understand or support their behavior. Caregivers of children will benefit from understanding that a child's fear, anxiety, hyper-activity, over-functioning, over-yielding, being loud, being quiet, risk-taking or cruelty to others actually makes sense in some way to the young person's brain or these behaviors would not be happening. Addictions and illegal behavior make sense to some aspect of the people who engage in these activities because everyone's thinking makes sense to them—or at least to a part of them.

Adults cannot assume that a child is thinking about a situation the way adults think about the same situation. Understanding how a young person's thinking and behavior makes sense to them is useful for helping them make better choices and coping with their challenges. Their words, emotions and behaviors reflect what kids have in their minds.

Tell me what you're thinking...

One of the simplest ways to discover a young person's thought process is to ask, "What are you thinking about _____? Simply, "Tell me what you're thinking," opens the door to making sense of the reaction, behavior or confusing responses adults can get from kids. Anyone who is patient enough to respectfully listen to another person's thought process, even if the viewpoint seems irrational at first hearing, will find something reasonable and rational behind the other's perspective, at least to them. This puts the listener in a better position to respond with truth and love rather than sarcasm, or some other negative response.

"Tell me what you are thinking," is an almost magical phrase for parenting and relating well to others. Conflictual logjams can often be sorted out by understanding what the other person believes behind their words and actions. The flames of conflict are fueled by reacting first and finding out the rationale behind a person's choices second. Instead, taking time to listen and genuinely appreciate the other person's thinking (even if it initially seems irrational to the listener) paves the way to conflict resolution. Even adolescents who engage in risky behavior have reasons for doing what they do.

The Teen Brain

Teens are growing rapidly and their brains are reorganizing for adulthood. During adolescence, the brain assesses what has been needed up to date and what is likely to be used in the future. If certain parts of the brain are not being used for their initial purposes, the brain reassigns brain real estate in preparation for adulthood. For example, the part of the brain that learns foreign languages will be made available for other purposes if the teen has not engaged in learning another language before adulthood. Adolescent brains are like homes under reconstruction—during a remodel living conditions are not the same, but the enhanced outcome is worth the temporary frustrations and inconvenience.

Adults benefit from understanding this frame of reference for the adolescent brain so they can respond to teenage behavior with insight and compassion. This does not mean adults are expected to excuse inappropriate or unsafe choices, but it does mean parents can react to teen words and behavior knowing in some way a teen's behavior makes logical, emotional sense to their restructuring brains.

Respectfully asking kids to clarify what they are thinking enables adults to understand why kids do what they do. Hard-to-understand behavior makes sense when viewed from the position of the one doing it. Sometimes what young people are doing is due to misinterpretation of what has been said in their hearing, sometimes young people know what adults don't know, and sometimes they remember what adults don't remember. Adults are not the only ones with correct understanding of situations. Kids' thinking usually makes sense when adults hear it from their perspectives because everyone's thinking makes sense to them.

The Menu Method

A common way adults have been trained to ask children about feelings is, "How does that make you feel?"

Common responses are shrugs, stares or "I don't know." These are typical replies from kids, whether they are young children or young adults. An opening question such as, "How does that make you feel?" may lead into a clear answer of a youngster's thoughts and feelings, but I have found young children through older teenagers generally find the question too broad and it does not help them filter through their feelings.

In addition to Hilton's Shame Barrel, another option for helping toddlers through twenty-somethings identify their thoughts and feelings is to give them choices. They often have an easier time selecting from a feelings menu than trying to generate their own descriptions of their emotional states. If a youngster lacks the sophistication or willingness to define feelings, it is still possible to gain understanding through a series of questions. I do this by offering feelings that would be common for most people their age who had similar experiences, such as, "A lot of kids would feel mad or sad if that happened to them. Did that make you feel mad or sad?"

A short answer from the youngster could be further clarified with another question like, "Was it more mad feelings or sad feelings?"

Through the simple process of basic choices and comparing one thought or feeling to another, we can learn what is going on inside youngsters and they can understand their emotional inner worlds more completely. By naming and fine-tuning feelings, young people can sift through the many emotions related to a situation. Sorting out these feelings helps people metabolize them.

One might suspect kids would give inaccurate answers if they are presented with only a short list of options about how they think or feel, but the opposite is generally true. Choices within a framework can be easier to evaluate than a broad, open-ended question. For example, a five-year-old will have an easier time answering the question, "Do you want spaghetti or chicken nuggets for lunch?" versus, "It's lunch time. What do you want?" Could a five-year-old spontaneously answer the question about their preference for lunch without choices? Of course, but the answer might be, "Cereal," everyday. Would it be easier for them to choose between alternatives? Usually the answer is yes. Choices do not eliminate the opportunity to expand or select something else. Instead, direct questions begin a discussion, which the participant can enter into.

People young and old are not overly conscious about their thinking as it relates to their circumstances, yet it is important to help clarify thinking because thoughts about a situation greatly impact how it is experienced. I see the power of this every day in my counseling practice. Life circumstances cause people to form beliefs about themselves and others, feelings follow thoughts, and clients continue to live out their ways of thinking regardless of whether their thinking is truthful or helpful. Imagine how unnecessary and disheartening it is for kids to spend many years living as if something were true and never finding out that their long held beliefs, upon which their lives have been built, are erroneous.

The menu method can also be used to identify feelings. Sometimes it is easier for people to identify their feelings rather than their thoughts. Some, though not all kids, can evaluate if they feel happy, sad, mad or afraid. These four emotions are like primary colors. They have many shades and subtleties, but mad, sad, glad and afraid are the core human emotions, in addition to shame. Generally offering mad, sad, happy and afraid as a beginning point opens the door for grasping a youngster's feelings.

The goal of the menu method is to discover what is going on inside young people in order to understand, correct their behavior or support them. Because everyone's thinking makes to them, it is useful to discover how kids are thinking and feeling behind the situations we find them in. Generally, on a continuum from easiest to hardest, the four basic feelings mentioned above can be the easiest menu to select from, followed by choices about thoughts. Finally, it is valuable to discover how kids think about themselves in their situations, which is a degree more sophisticated than discovering what kids are thinking and feeling. It can be more challenging for young people to identify how they think about themselves in various situations, but a series of questions helps them here, too. Specific questions help determine if something is true, false, or somewhere in between.

Generally, I frame questions about self with yes or no questions such as, "Did the problem of _____ make you think *I am bad* or did you feel responsible in some way because this happened?" Each of these questions causes the youngster to evaluate if some or all of the statements being offered are true. It's not uncommon for an adult to answer, "Of course I'm responsible for it. I'm responsible for everything!" A reply like this is usually coupled with a chuckle which belies their tendency to take responsibility for more than their share of life. Another typical response from an adult might be quiet, internal evaluation, followed by a statement such as, "I do feel badly about what happened, but I didn't cause it and there is no way I could have stopped it so I'm not blaming myself." This type of complex, sophisticated clarity is not always available to young people, so brief yes or no questions about possible ideas regarding their self-identity open the door to self-discovery and discussion.

Another question, "Do you think I'm not lovable because the bad thing happened?" is also met with nods or a straightforward yes or no according to the youngster's internal truth.

Asking kids, "Do you think you made something about the bad thing happen?" is almost always greeted with an affirmative response. Suggesting possible thoughts which might be related to their circumstances helps young people start to evaluate how their thinking—accurate or erroneous—contributes to their understanding and reaction.

Younger children give less complex replies to questions about themselves. The question, "Did the problem _____ make you think *I am bad*?" is often met with a sullen nod or quiet yes. Usually negative experiences generate negative beliefs, and often negative or erroneous beliefs about the self. It can be painful for youngsters to acknowledge negative thoughts and feelings due to the underlying shame that can accompany negative experiences. Yet self-identity is at the heart of why kids get stuck; therefore, identifying their internal self-beliefs is key to helping young people rebound from challenges. This intervention has the power to change their behavior.

Note that the above question—*Did the problem make you think I am bad?*—is phrased in first person, making it easy for a youngster to determine if it is the right one for them. It is counter-intuitive to state a question about someone else in the framework of an *I*-statement, but the effect for the client is quite noticeable and appears easier to metabolize. Phrases such as, "Did the situation make you think you are bad?" Or, "Do you feel like a loser?" can suggest *you are bad* and *you are a loser*. Even though it is subtle, the grammatically correct question that includes *you* causes people to unconsciously defend themselves or brace for further criticism. It may unnecessarily validate a negative view they already have about themselves.

Deliberately turning a question around to include an *I*-statement gives the listener a chance to consider the statement without suggesting it is true. Questions like these would fail English and grammar exams, but I find people—children through adults —do not get confused about the purpose or subject of a question with an "*I*" statement in it.

Examples of questions about the other person with an "*I*" statement are:

- When you didn't get invited to the slumber party did you think *what's wrong with me?*

- Because your team won the state basketball tournament did you start believing *I rock when it comes to basketball? I'm a really good person.* (The danger of this viewpoint is that the win is very contextual and does not actually apply to a person's self-worth.)

- After last night's game did you start thinking *I missed the winning point and now everybody will hate me? I'm terrible.*

- When your mom and dad got divorced did you think *I'm not as good as other kids whose parents aren't divorced?*

It takes a bit of practice to flip questions around before asking them this way, but it is worth the effort. Doing so will make sense to the listener and avoid criticizing them in the process.

People of all ages do not tire of someone's genuine desire to understand how they think and feel. Others usually find it quite helpful to have another person engage them in sorting through their thoughts and emotions. By responding to a menu of yes or no questions, young people usually discover there are more layers of feelings and thoughts than they originally guessed. Sifting through these, and framing them with comparative questions, usually helps kids clarify the nature of their concerns, including their mental and emotional responses.

All grownups—parents, teachers, babysitters, friends and professionals—can help young people clarify their thoughts and feelings, which is a preliminary approach to helping kids make sense of their circumstances. Once thoughts, feelings and *I am* statements are clarified, young people are on their way to addressing problems in an empowered way. Validation is another response that further equips kids. Virtually every person benefits from validation and anyone can do it.

2. *VALIDATION*

Validation is like giving away free money. Everybody likes it. It is the second step in helping young people think correctly after adults help youngsters clarify what they are feeling and believing. As a next step, validation affirms they are good, their thoughts and feelings matter, and their perspective makes sense.

When I first began my role as a professional counselor, I found myself saying to many people, "This feels bad because it is bad."

"Really?" they would ask incredulously. "Do you think it's reasonable I'm upset about this?"

"Yes," I answered. "Anyone would feel badly about what you're going through…(divorce, parents fighting, harassment, a difficult move, being left out at school, etc.)."

"Do you really think so?" they often asked again, needing reassurance that they were not lacking some supernatural backbone other people have for weathering life's challenges.

"Yes, I really think so," I reassured them. "This feels bad because it is bad."

People do not outgrow the need to be validated for what they are thinking and feeling. We might assume adults, who have more years of life experience than young people, would not need the same degree of understanding reflected back to them, but no one graduates from the need to be understood. With care and sensitive truth, it is very useful to reflect back to people of all ages what they are going through.

Young people especially find it quite helpful to receive some degree of reinforcement that what they are facing, feeling, and thinking is normal. It is meaningful to hear that someone else in their shoes would think and feel the same way—at least in part. There is almost always some way to validate another person. If a parent comes home and finds teenage boys doing flips off the third story roof onto mattresses, a parent can say, "I know this seems like a good way to practice your snowboard jumps, but it's too dangerous." This comment validates the desire, but redirects the action.

As part of helping young people process their thoughts and feelings, validation gives them assurance that their emotions and ideas matter. Validation means there is something normal, common, or legitimate—from their viewpoint—in what a person is doing or saying. It is verification that their thoughts, feelings, wishes, or needs are worthy of being understood. Affirming the normalcy of a reaction and the difficulty of a situation gives people a stronger foundation for facing what they have to face. Validation does not mean a person is without erroneous thinking or excessive emotion. Validation means other people, in the same situation, might feel similarly to them and their feelings and perspectives have value.

Families bring challenging kids to therapy with the hope a counselor can get their son or daughter to line up with a parents' viewpoint. There are good reasons to involve a counselor in helping a family solve problems, but seldom is one family member completely right and the other family members completely wrong. Part of the work with families is to find ways to validate each person, including a frustrated teen, a discouraged single mom, or an angry stepparent because everyone's thinking makes sense to them. It even makes sense to other people when it is understood.

Two parents and a 16-year-old daughter came to my office and said the same things over and over to each other and me. The father wanted his daughter to be stronger and more resilient yet the daughter was overwhelmed by her commitment to play on an elite volleyball team, take advanced placement classes and participate in orchestra. The mother feared that if her daughter did not continue with each of her many activities at a high level she might not get into the college of her choice. The daughter was becoming depressed.

In the beginning of our work together, my job with the family was to validate what I could support about each person's view and to point out that the daughter was using increasingly extreme measures to get a message to her parents. I validated that each parent wanted something good for their daughter and they were afraid about her opportunities if she decreased her involvement in any of her many activities. I pointed out that the daughter was in fear of disappointing them. At the same time, I confirmed how overwhelming her schedule would be for anyone. The conflict over the daughter's life began to shift as I stated, as clearly as I could, that each person's motive was positive. I reinforced that they were trying hard to make life okay for themselves and each other.

Unfortunately, though, life was becoming quite difficult for the daughter and she was cutting herself. She was struggling with low self-esteem, adolescent social drama and very high pressure to achieve. The parents wanted their daughter to keep achieving at the level they desired, but without the problem of cutting. I validated what was true for each of them, even though I did not agree with each of their perspectives. It was easy to validate their motives because they loved their daughter. Yet they each had an agenda, which was contributing to the problem. We gained traction after each person felt that their perspective, to some degree, was legitimate. Validation broke the logjam and led into problem-solving.

When people are validated, they usually display some type of visual relief by sighing, posture shifts, or a remark like, "You can't believe how helpful it is to hear you say that." Validation is so helpful to youngsters they almost always respond in a way which prompts the speaker to repeat the validation. They will often stop what they are doing and make direct eye contact to see if what is being said to them is true.

"Really?" is one of the most common phrases I hear from younger kids when they have been validated, which evokes a repeat of the assurance they have just been given. It means they want to test whether the speaker is teasing or lying to them.

Many people need validation that what they are experiencing is normal and others would feel and think the same way in their situation. Once again, validation does not mean agreement with everything another person is thinking or doing. Validation confirms that a young person's viewpoint is important and can be understood in context, which often leads to some flexibility between conflictual parties. Validating phrases include statements like *you probably think I don't understand...*, *I know you've calculated how you can go to soccer camp and participate in an adventure trip...*, *it makes sense you want_____; need_____; think I should _____*, etc.

Almost every situation has some aspect which can be validated from the lens of the person in the situation. Validation enables people to move on to sorting out what is true and which steps need to be taken. Without validation, people work hard to maintain their positions in order to feel understood. The skill of validation will be further discussed in the *Perspectives* section with successful parenting strategies.

3. TRUTH AND POWER

Once thoughts and feelings have been understood and validated, the third step in addressing what kids believe is helping them understand truth about themselves and their circumstances. As part of revealing truth, young people need to know who has power in their lives to solve problems and meet their needs. The issues of truth and power are so straightforward for adults they tend to assume young people see situations the way adults see them. Therefore, adults can fail to give youngsters much needed guidance around truth and power—information which has the capability to change their worlds. This message is the purpose of this book. If we know what young people are thinking—which may be surprising when we take the time to discover it—we can offer information to help young people understand what is true about themselves and their environments. When truth and power have been identified, solutions often present themselves and youngsters get relief.

TRUTH

In review, young people of all ages derive meaning about themselves from what happens to and around them. They use their young minds to understand situations and they believe their understanding is accurate. Yet young children through late adolescents generally do not have enough information and mature thinking to make correct judgments about themselves and their circumstances. Through their inaccurate perceptions, kids make up their own meaning about themselves, their situations, their families and their futures. Young people assume what they believe is true, but in many cases, it is not.

Truth could be summarized as accuracy. One way we can help kids understand life correctly is to share accurate information with them. Accurate information includes how much things cost, who has responsibility in various situations, what is expected of kids, what young people can expect of others, what has happened, what will happen, and the nature of circumstances in which youngsters find themselves. Accurate and age-appropriate information gives young people relief. It enables them to understand themselves and their situations from a broader, more complex perspective than they can generate on their own. Ideally, accurate information should help kids and not shame them.

Young people of all ages benefit when adults offer mature, accurate thinking instead of the uninformed, immature and sometimes emotionally-driven thinking of kids. For example, youngsters pick up distress in their families and wonder if their parents are going to divorce, or they know one parent has lost a job and the partner is upset. Children wonder what will happen to their families in such a case, and they can easily misinterpret situations unless someone helps them understand. Giving young people appropriate truth includes the amount of honest information that will help them cope with what is happening, at the same time relieving them from the responsibility to solve adult problems. Here again, the positive truth about kids' identities is one of the most useful pieces of truth young people need when family situations are out of equilibrium. Accurate information about a youngster's self-identity and how the family will continue to meet the young person's needs are paramount during change.

For example, a family's move from one state to another could be handled by explaining to a young person why the family is moving, how the family will address the challenges of leaving friends, and that they will make new friends in the new school and neighborhood. A youngster might respond to this future forecast with doubt and disappointment, but a parent can say, "I know you don't believe me now, but I think you'll be playing with new kids pretty soon after we get to our new place. I am confident you'll have another best friend not too long after that." The young person might not give any visible sign this information is helpful, but they will hold onto it with the hope the parent is correct. If the statement is underwritten by legitimate truth, it will be a strong resource to the young person who has to make unwanted changes.

A positive and plausible outcome about what might happen in the future is quite helpful to kids of all ages. Yet truth is only appropriate if it is helpful. A child who struggles to find playmates in one state may struggle in the next location, in which case an inaccurate future forecast would be hurtful.

Not all truth is helpful to children. Young people are helped by information which enables them to feel safe, understood, and to know their places in various situations. The following criteria expand on aspects of appropriate truth.

Truth is Related to Context
Useful truth includes attunement to a child's age and circumstances. It considers the time, place and situation surrounding the receiver. For example, the time to give direct, difficult feedback to a teenage daughter is not while a parent is driving her with friends to an outing. Information in that setting will be potentially shaming and embarrassing. The same message can be shared at bedtime, after dinner, or when the teen is alone.

Appropriate truth should relate to the listener for the listener's age and development. Telling a disappointed 15-year-old who did not get selected for the school play he has the intelligence to grow up and be a doctor might be true, but it is not fitting or useful for the adolescent's immediate context. The disappointment of not being selected for a desired opportunity cannot be mitigated by the projection of success later in life—even if the projection is accurate. Such a response from an adult suggests the adult undervalues the disappointment a teen is experiencing in the present. Appropriate truth can include a positive projection of what might happen in the future, but it is ideally related to what is important to the young person at the time.

Not being invited to birthday parties in elementary school is disappointing for many kids. In such a case, contextual, appropriate truth could be, "I know it feels bad to not get invited to a party. Sometimes you get invited to parties and sometimes other kids get invited. It's more fun to be invited though and I know you're disappointed." This example includes validation, understanding how the young person feels, and the truth that not being invited to parties happens to most people at some time or another.

Truth without sensitivity to the needs of the child, even if it is accurate, is not always helpful. Timing and consideration of the young person's mood, circumstances, and capability for hearing should be factored into sharing truth with kids.

Truth is for the Benefit of the Young Person

Humans of all ages need understanding, validation, and truth which takes seriously what they are experiencing at each stage of life. Adults can find it difficult to take seriously what is important to youngsters. Caregivers may want to bypass the joys and agonies of youth and give kids a perspective more important to the adult world than the world of young people. Appropriate truth needs to be geared to the maturity and context of the youngster who is hearing it.

For example, I suggested a version of appropriate truth for Cynthia, an adult client who was raising teenagers. Cynthia replied, "When I told my mom what was going on for me in the drama of the teenage years she often said, 'I wouldn't be your age again for anything.' I'm sure it was true for her but not very helpful to me."

Cynthia did not benefit as a teenager from her mother's remarks because the words implied *it sucks to be a teenager* yet Cynthia was a teenager at the time. In order for truth to be useful to young people it has to be comprised of messages which will help them, either in the present or for the future, and not primarily about an adult who is remembering their own childhood. Not all truth is helpful.

Truth Should be Selective

Parents need discernment when offering truth. How much information adults share, and how many words they use to share it, depend on the age and circumstances of the listener. The window for speaking to youngsters and their capacity to absorb what is being said varies from year to year. As parents of adolescents know, a younger child may be more inclined to listen to a parent's thoughts than a teenager, although a few words aptly spoken to a teen can be very influential. Caregivers are wise to consider a young person's readiness for hearing what they have to say. Because truth is for the benefit of the young person, it should reflect the youngster's capacity for hearing and not the caregiver's need for talking. When adults offer truth to adolescents, it is generally important to spend time listening and let a few wise words serve their purpose rather than argue or try to convince a younger person about an adult's perspective.

Selective, honest input improves children's lives and should be an intentional process. Adults face challenges beyond the scope of kids. Ideal sharing means parents don't communicate too much about parental concerns with younger family members. What may seem manageable to adults can be misunderstood or be too weighty for kids to carry. Oversharing adult problems with young people inadvertently enlists them to right the ship of their families and take on responsibilities that may be too burdensome for them to handle.

The following are examples of selective sharing that will help a young person while being appropriate to the context:

71

- Telling kids that their parents' divorce is not caused by anything the kids have done and withholding information that would negatively influence their view of the other parent.

- Telling a young adopted child she has not done anything wrong to cause her to go to the other parent's house for a week. Instead, it is a rule the courts made so the mommy and the daddy could both love and take care of her.

- Telling a teen in front of his friend that it won't work out for him to go on a spring break ski trip and privately sharing the related, appropriate financial facts later.

- Telling a family member about an upcoming move or loss of a job, but not burdening the young person with the adult's need for emotional support.

Appropriate truth takes into account the needs of young people and protects them from information which can be unnecessarily hurtful, inaccurate or too weighty for them to handle.

Truth Can Be Authoritative

Appropriate truth helps young people gain perspective about situations, themselves and others. Very often, young people cannot find truth themselves because they do not have enough maturity to discern it. Sometimes appropriate truth is parental authority.

This example from our family illustrates what I believe is appropriate, parental truth. When our son Tim was 13 years old, his team lost a close soccer game. In spite of personally scoring three goals, Tim was beside himself with anger and disappointment. I let him blow off steam for a few minutes, but his meltdown continued. I was facing a car ride home with an unpleasant teenager until I gave him a bit of appropriate truth. I said he would play many soccer games in his life and if he could not win and lose with a respectable attitude he would not be able to play soccer. I asked him to get himself together before we drove home. I reminded Tim that soccer is a recreational activity and only one aspect of his life. He needed to find a way to win or lose with a decent attitude or he could not play soccer.

Many years later, Tim reported that was a pivotal conversation for him. He said it made soccer more fun because he could give his best in a game and enjoy the rest of the day whether his team won or lost.

Truth can be, "No means no, and I'm not going to change my mind," or "I am not comfortable with what you're planning, so I can't say yes." The answers of yes and no can be authoritative, appropriate truth.

Parents and other adults must accept the responsibility to be more than people-pleasers if they are going to give young people what they really need—guidance for growing and successfully living in a larger world. With good judgment, attunement to young people requires adults to hold good boundaries, and field kids' emotions without sacrificing wisdom. Requiring children to have appropriate behavior requires appropriate truth, which can occasionally be difficult to deliver yet vital for the well-being of young people.

Truth Can Mean "I'm Sorry"

Truth coming from a caregiver is sometimes, "I'm sorry." Truth may also be pointing out that a young person needs to acknowledge they have done something wrong. Kids learn social behavior in their home environments. Admitting one is wrong and specifically naming the wrong actions or words is mature, socially appropriate behavior. Young people need to learn this skill and trusted adults around them are the best teachers by example and instruction. Kids can be coached in the right way to admit a wrong by the parent to whom the words need to be spoken. This intervention is as simple as a parent saying, "I know we were upset with each other last night, but you said some very hurtful words to me. I am asking you to admit what you did was wrong." If the parent is at fault, they can admit wrong and apologize by saying, "It was wrong of me to_____, and I'm sorry." This adult behavior models how to take responsibility for one's behavior and choices.

I am intentionally suggesting kids be coached to admit wrong-doing rather than apologize with an insincere "I'm sorry." Caregivers may want to require a young person to apologize for unacceptable behavior, but a more organic reality is that kids need to know what they have done wrong, accept responsibility for it and admit their mistakes. A spontaneous apology that follows the admission of wrong is acceptable, but children cannot be forced into being regretful. Requiring them to say, "I'm sorry," when they actually have no remorse is false and counter-productive. Kids can be required to recognize what is wrong with their behavior and guided to take responsibility for it, with the phrase, "It was wrong for me to (fill in the problem)."

Truth Reveals Who Owns the Problem

A simple formula provides wisdom for life: *Don't take the problem if you don't have the power.* How often do we encounter people who are highly distressed about situations over which they have no control? Adults discuss small and large problems in the world, generally knowing they do not have the power to resolve any of the situations discussed. Adults enter this process with an understanding problems will be unresolved when the conversations end and adults return to their personal matters. They understand the relationship between problems and power.

In contrast, kids, due to their immaturity and lack of understanding, take on many problems they cannot change and continue to worry over many issues. Youngsters of all ages worry about other kid's problems and events in the media. They feel concern for their parents when they hear about difficult scenarios that no one helps them understand. It is common for school age children to be quite concerned for other kids who are being teased or treated harshly by adults. It is normal for adolescents to not understand why their parents do what they do. Because young people do not have the maturity to accurately perceive the scope of situations or to understand that some problems cannot be remedied, kids of all ages are distressed by the difficulties around them. Unlike seasoned adults who understand the scope and inevitability of troubles, youngsters can be very affected by circumstances they cannot change until someone helps them understand what is happening and who has the power to address it.

I observe that adults are generally unaware kids are distressed about situations grownups accept as part of life. Adults know some situations resolve themselves, people outgrow difficulties, and action steps can be taken to handle problems. Kids may not know these truths unless they are told what is happening and what to expect. Without information, youngsters can be very concerned about problems, but be too immature to grasp what the problem means and who will handle its resolution.

One of the most impactful conversations adults can offer young people regards who has power in the various circumstances in which kids find themselves. Relieving young people of unnecessary responsibility, and providing them with helpful truth, lets kids be kids while they are young.

The Value of Truth

In addition to helping young people clarify their thoughts and feelings, giving them accurate truth is an intervention which can change their lives for the better if adults are mindful about what hurts and what helps kids. Parents and other adults are in critical positions to insert truth about young people's identities, values, skills and futures. Words spoken to young people can stay with them for a lifetime and influence their success and satisfaction in the world. Without appropriate truth, young people of all ages make sense of the world with immature thinking. Children have difficulty understanding that sometimes the hardest things in life turn out okay. Setting young people up for success often requires sharing adult wisdom with them regarding what is happening, what will happen, and what it means for kids personally.

Because the outside world is constantly entering the inside world of young people, caregivers can intentionally add valuable messages to this intake process, knowing that most of what adults say will eventually have some impact on the kids in their care.

Our adult daughter Kelly said one of the most helpful things I did as a parent was telling her every day in middle school there was nothing wrong with her, everyone felt as insecure as she did, and most people, like her, would outgrow this phase of life. She was referencing the truth I offered her when she was 12 through 16 years old.

As a middle school student, Kelly said to me, "It doesn't seem like everyone feels as insecure as I do. I don't believe you, but will you tell me this every day?"

I gladly accepted her request. Almost daily, I reminded her she was a fine person and she and her peer group would mature beyond the insecurities of early adolescence. I repeated she was normal, everyone around her felt insecure, and life would not always be like it was in middle school. It was easy to say because it was true. I was lending Kelly an adult perspective she could not perceive on her own because she did not have the maturity and the lens to see herself and the situation accurately. By transferring a truth, I was assuring Kelly she had worth and predicting that she would outgrow the insecurity of young adolescence. Later, when Kelly was in college, she commented that the truth I offered her in middle school was one of the most helpful things she experienced in her teenage years.

Parents complain that their children do not listen to them. The truth is youngsters are listening all the time to the words, actions and emotional tone of caregivers to determine their own value and worth. Adults who carefully insert positive truth into the lives of young people will support their journeys toward being healthy adults. Reflecting strengths, talents, capabilities and positive futures to young people is like pouring wet cement—it sets over time and creates a lasting foundation.

Harmful Information

There is a version of sharing which is the opposite of the appropriate truth mentioned above. Some information is more than can be metabolized at a young person's age and maturity even if it is accurate. Unnecessarily giving kids honest information can demean, shame or negatively influence them regarding themselves or important others if the negative information does not consider the needs of the young listener. This type of 'truth' is often a projection of the speaker's distress and can hurt kids more than it helps them. Harmful words are better left unsaid because there are no word erasers in the world to take away the impact of unnecessarily hurtful statements. Matter-of-fact statements which are not accurate or helpful leave an impression that lingers in the mind of the listener—often for a lifetime.

Statements like "You're so lazy you probably won't graduate from high school," imprint on young people's psyches as truth and can run like computer programs, especially if they are spoken with intensity and repeated. Kids believe all types of 'truth' they hear because young people tend to believe what they are told. Just as we cannot un-ring a bell, we cannot guarantee the effects of inappropriate words spoken to kids can be undone. Whenever possible, it is wise to refrain from sharing harmful statements with kids, or to later retract hurtful comments spoken in frustration and fear.

I observed an interaction in a grocery store, which was probably meant to be funny, but I am not sure all the participants found it humorous or understood its meaning. A stranger casually said to a mother with two children around three years old, "I see you have twins."

"Yes," the mother replied. "Would you like one?"

Children of this age understand language well enough to interpret the actual word exchange, but they may not be sophisticated enough to read the humor or nuanced meaning in their mother's reply. I assume the mother was using code to say *yes, I do have twins and it's a lot of work. I could use some relief.* I also assume she loved her twins and would not actually give one of them away. This exchange in the store is exactly the circumstance which can be interpreted as humorous to adults and frightening to kids. It is likely the mother used this phrase many times in the children's hearing. Humorous or not, it may leave an impression in the youngsters who overhear it. Remember, many three-year-olds whole-heartedly believe Santa Claus brings them presents because they take words at face value. If the mother enjoyed using the phrase of offering to give away one of her children, she could have taken a moment to reassure her twins she would never actually give them away because she loved them both very much. Without clarification, the mother's offer to give away one of her kids may have been confusing because the comment contained some element of underlying truth in it related to the fatigue and challenge of raising twins—concepts too sophisticated for the youngsters to correctly interpret.

Harmful, inappropriate phrases thrust at young people are comments like:

- "I wish I never had you. Why did I ever have kids?"
- "You screw up everything you do. Why can't you read (swim, succeed, etc.) like other kids?"

- "Do you know how much money I spend for...?" accompanied by shame and anger.
- "Mommy used to be fun before you came along."
- "You're the problem here."

Comments like these, especially when expressed with strong emotion, leave an impression that does not easily dissipate when the tense moment has passed. Kids believe what they hear, especially when it is repeated. Ideally, adults would be careful about how they share their difficulties with young people. Done correctly, sharing feelings can be valuable role modeling of emotional processing, but expressing upset feelings as definitive statements or hurtful words about other people is damaging and may leave an impact. The following are alternative words to express the true feelings within the negative messages above.

- "I wish I never had you. Why did I ever have kids?"
Alternative: "You can tell I'm frustrated right now. I'm upset about things at work and that you and your brother didn't do your chores when you got home from school. I'm hungry, just like you are, but I can't cook dinner until the two of you put the dishes in the dishwasher."

- "You screw up everything you do. Why can't you read, (swim, succeed, etc.) like other kids?"
Alternative: "I can tell you are having a hard time and I'm sorry. Everybody struggles sometimes. What's going on?"

- "Do you know how much money I spend for...?"
Alternative: "I'm glad you're taking trumpet lessons, and I know you have musical talent, but I'm not going to keep paying for your lessons if you are not committed to practicing. Because you don't practice and you're uncooperative about going to lessons, it's time to take a break." A child hearing these phrases might be disappointed, angry or relieved, which an adult can help process without changing their position on the cost or effectiveness of the lessons.

- "You're the problem here."
Alternative: "We've got a problem here and we have to find

a solution. The problem is _(statement of the problem)_ and we need to fix it. What are your ideas? I am going to share my ideas as well."

The above harmful comments and their alternatives are a small sampling of what adults say to young people. Unloading unnecessary negative comments on kids leaves them with emotional residue long after remarks have been made. Inappropriate statements linger in children's psyches and make them doubt their value and worth. Adults in my clinical practice are still referring to the negative statements made about them in childhood. Negative remarks thrust at children as 'truth' have the power to indelibly stamp kids with a negative identity. Appropriate truth helps young people develop according to their true potential, identities, and skills. Negative 'truth' creates the opposite effect.

POWER

Unveiling where the power lies in various circumstances relieves young people of burdens adults may not know kids are carrying. Adults have to interpret for kids where kids have power and where they do not. Adults create safety and peace by explicitly telling young people the scope of their responsibilities and what belongs in the hands of grownups.

In difficult circumstances, young people need to be informed about who has responsibility and power. Without correct information, kids carry others' distress in their young hearts and minds. When young people are appropriately informed, they usually drop much of the distress they are carrying. They are relieved when adults clarify for them the nature of what is happening around them and what is likely to happen in the future.

For example, youngsters can be very impacted by an adult's harsh treatment of another person. Kids come home from school quite concerned about conflict in the classroom or the needs of other kids. Many young people over-identify with another person's distress. They worry and want to solve another person's problem until they have information about the situation and are assured that a capable adult is addressing the other person's needs.

Explaining what is likely to happen in the future for someone else is very beneficial information for young people who are impacted by, but cannot relieve, the distress around them.

Addressing the issue of power, as I am suggesting it here, involves adults explaining to young people what adults are responsible to handle and what responsibilities are in the hands of kids. I hear from young people in my counseling practice that they are very concerned about problems in their families, but they do not have any reassurance capable adults are handling the problems. Sometimes a youngster's angst occurs because they do not understand what's happening and why adults are not seemingly addressing the problem. Young people will try to handle problems or carry another's angst in their own bodies until they understand a situation from a more accurate position.

For example, parents with a new baby may choose to let an infant cry until it falls asleep on its own. A three-year-old in the room next door may be very concerned because no one is helping the baby feel better, which the three-year-old would want if they were crying. Without an explanation, a three-year-old might suggest, "We have to see what's wrong with the baby," "I'm afraid the baby is hurt," or "Maybe I should give the baby my blanket."

A three-year-old's distress can be relieved by telling them grownups are taking care of the problem and explaining the situation in an appropriate way, such as, "Everything is okay with the baby. She has a full tummy and she is very tired. The best place for her to fall asleep is in her bed, which she will probably do in a few moments. If she's still crying in a few minutes I will go in and check on her."

The emotional vibration of distress resonates in the bodies of those near people in pain, but most adults can choose how to respond to it. Kids hear babies crying, parents fighting, neighbors yelling, other youngsters being punished, authorities removing kids from abusive homes and more. The emotional impact of these occurrences is significant. Most often kids do not have the power to make a difference for the person hurting, but they have secondary impact from the problem. Interpreting the situation to a young person in an age-appropriate way, and stating who has the power within the problem, gives kids tremendous relief. Without an opportunity to understand correctly what is happening around them, young people of all ages can carry another person's distress in their bodies and bear responsibility for situations beyond their scope to handle.

A young mother told me about being in the car with her five-year-old son who heard a story on the radio about a young child who needed adoption. The announcer described the needs of the boy and the five-year-old said, "We could adopt him and I could play with him. He could have some of my toys." Her son was responding to the other child's distress because it activated compassion in his heart, but as a child he did not have the power to address the other youngster's needs. The parent reassured her son about how grownups would take care of the boy.

An attuned parent can see the ripple of relief flow through young people when they understand what is happening and who is handling a problem. Kids are affected by circumstances around them and they may not perceive the limits of their power to solve problems. With adult guidance, young people can be free to focus attention on their own lives and respond to the needs of others when appropriate.

Adults Solving Problems

When young people make mistakes or create bad situations for themselves and others, they need clarification about which part of the problem is theirs to resolve and which part can only be handled by adults. Kids can create problems beyond their capacity to solve them. Accidently injuring another child, unintentionally separating from a parent in a public setting, or damaging another person's property are examples of problems young people create without having the power to solve them.

The person with the power should solve a problem. One of the most powerful and consistently appropriate statements to offer a young person is, "This is a grownup problem and grownups are going to handle it." Whether it is divorce, something significant with another child, or a concern specific to the youngster, being told that grownups understand the problem and are going to bring their resources to solving it is a message kids need to hear. Young people can create problems for themselves and others, but seldom can they be the sole agents of resolution. When adults understand problems that affect children and assure them solving the problem is possible and will be guided by safe adults, kids usually release the burdens they are carrying. Assurance that adults are handling a problem is especially relieving to overly-responsible, sensitive youngsters. It is almost a magical phrase.

For example, a first driving accident is usually handled by parents and teens. Teens should call the appropriate authorities when an accident takes place, but they usually do not have the power to compensate for damages caused by an accident. When teens try to hide their accidents or avoid telling parents about legal matters, the aftermath is usually more complicated than if adults had been involved from the beginning. Adults can simultaneously be very frustrated about situations kids create yet reassure youngsters adults will be appropriately involved in solving teen problems. Car accidents usually are a grownup problem, as well as other situations kids can get themselves into without their own power of resolution.

Sometimes kids have the power to solve problems, but often they do not. For example, a child who takes money out of another student's desk can be directed to return the money and admit they did something wrong. An adult can oversee this interaction, but the young person takes the action steps. In contrast, teenagers who deface property or break into a building may face police involvement, which merits the maturity and resources of adults, as well as the responsible restitution and consequences paid by the teens. In short, it is important for adults to help kids when they are over their heads and for young people to learn appropriate responsibility at every age.

This is a grownup problem is such a potent truth for young people that I use it often in my counseling practice. This phrase is powerful for two reasons: 1) It is true and people can metabolize the truth (something untrue is very hard to digest), and 2) It creates safety for kids and promises their positive value is still intact even though something negative has happened.

Kids Solving Problems

Many problems are within the scope of kids' power to resolve. Young people need to be the ones admitting wrong, taking responsibility for their mistakes and taking right actions. An adult stepping in to defend a young person who is in the wrong hinders the young person's development. Adults inappropriately assigning blame to others, such as a teacher, when a student is at fault, stunts the maturation and growth of kids. Knowing where responsibility lies and clarifying it, are vital components for helping young people become high functioning people.

Kids can solve their own problems and be coached about what to do in various situations. For example, adults can script words young people need to say and stand by when children have to apologize. Parents can respectfully talk with kids about their roles in problems and brainstorm potential solutions so young people can navigate their situations. Difficulties overseen by adults and managed by kids can be vital opportunities for young people to grow. In many cases, kids need to address kid problems under the auspices of healthy adults.

Parents' anxiety can prevent young people from handling situations they need to handle. Parents need to manage not getting their own emotional relief about a problem because their children need to handle a problem first. I observe this for parents with kids of all ages. For example, one mom sent her high school senior for a weekend trip across the country to visit a college friend because the daughter had not been invited to prom. The girl had a prom dress with matching shoes and bag hanging in her closet waiting for a prom invitation. When a date did not materialize, the mother spent additional funds on a weekend cross country trip so her daughter would not be too upset. The college student was burdened by the presence of her high school friend, which I suspect was occurring to lower the mother's distress. Rather than help her high school daughter find solutions, the mom spent a good deal of money lowering her own anxiety.

Kids' problems cause parents pain. Knowing what to do with that pain is important. There are situations young people need to handle and adults are their best teachers. In order to be helpful, caregivers need to have their own emotional intelligence —the ability to manage disappointment and frustration—in order to equip young people to think through and solve problems. Caregivers over-responding by contacting teachers, haranguing coaches, and over-paying for solutions instead of weathering their own distress can be detrimental to young people. Instead, when parents hear a young person's distressing report, it is useful to gather the scope of the problem as much as possible, clarify the young person's role, and empower them to address the situation and grow from it. Stepping in to solve problems for kids too soon, rather than enabling them to learn from problems and develop coping skills, hinders them from maturing. Clarifying when adults hold power and equipping young people to successfully take ownership, helps them grow.

PUTTING TRUTH AND POWER TOGETHER

The two most powerful responses for helping kids with appropriate truth are 1) telling them in age-appropriate language what is actually happening to and around them so they can process it correctly, and 2) communicating who has the power in a situation, including what the young person's role will be in the circumstance. Kids pick up many messages in what is happening around them. Useful truth validates what they see and hear, while assuring them adults are aware of their situations and will use appropriate adult power.

The following are examples of sharing truth with kids and helping them understand who has the power within the problem.

- The world history teacher in a high school is very demanding and has poor social skills when interacting with students. He is four years from retirement. A sophomore student may be very frustrated that Mr. Winslow gives them too much homework and disregards the student's other school commitments. After parents validate the student's frustration, useful truth may include that the school administration has received complaints about him before, has dealt with the problem in their way, Mr. Winslow is not very likely to change, and Mr. Winslow will

84

probably teach in the high school four more years until he retires. These truths suggest that the student has to make adjustments to the situation because it is not likely to change. The student may not like hearing this truth, especially if he or she would like to go the administration with parents and complain about Mr. Winslow. Knowing the problem cannot be solved in the way the student would like it to be, they can develop the ability to do the homework assigned as other students do, accept that the situation will not change, and find a way to successfully finish the term. Acceptance and personal change can be the most effective response to difficulties.

• A teenage daughter is hurt by the social drama of her peers. Truth entails non-shaming honesty about the girl's participation in social drama, validation that this type of behavior is hurtful but common in adolescence, and shared problem-solving between the adolescent and compassionate adults. This is the kind of help that empowers students. Appropriate truth entails validating that gossip feels bad, being reminded that many teenagers outgrow this unkind behavior, and power lies in not participating in hurtful gossip. Empowerment in this scenario primarily falls in the student's realm, where she can be intentional about choosing a circle of friends based on character and trustworthiness.

• A significant loss may be occurring for a child or family, such as the loss of a pet, a move away from friends, a major illness, or other challenges. Sharing truth is to explain what is happening, who has responsibility to address the challenges, and what will probably happen in the future. Information is power and it is a defense against the difficult, unchangeable and unfortunate situations young people have to face.

An adult's story underscores the theme of truth and power. Franco came to therapy to address a profound sorrow he had carried since young childhood, which was diagnosed by his psychiatrist. As we debriefed the session, Franco said, "When my parents argued, they validated they were upset and they reassured us they would work it out and stay together, which they did. They never talked to us about the conflict between my dad and my older brother. My brother and my dad fought a lot, but they didn't talk to us about it. I didn't worry about my mom and dad, but I worried about my brother. I've carried that sadness inside me for 25 years."

Franco's parents were wise to give him the truth about their marital conflict and the reassurance they had the power to stay together in spite of how their conflict appeared to him as a child. These two pieces of information enabled him not to worry. Without the reassurance about truth and power regarding Franco's brother, Franco worried over someone he loved and carried that sorrow into adulthood. Franco's parents probably assumed the brother would outgrow his conflictual behavior and it did not occur to them that Franco would be troubled and worried about their conflicts, even though it was a significant source of stress for him. Franco's parents could have resolved this distress for Franco as well with a brief discussion about the truth and power of the situation.

Twenty-five-year-old Chamberlain shared the story about the death of his father when he was three years old. Chamberlain's father was killed in an automobile accident and within a year his mother married an alcoholic. Chamberlain tried to manage life in the midst of their violent and raging episodes. Chamberlain described himself, his household, and his life with the word *pathetic*.

"I came to believe I was pathetic," he said. "My life and family were pathetic so I assumed I was pathetic as a result of it all."

I replied, "What would it have been like for you if an adult had said, '*This is a really tough situation, but none of it is your fault? What's happening at your house is nothing about you and you can't fix it. You're a little boy inside a big problem and only grownups can fix the problem. There is nothing you can do to make this better and I'm sorry it is so hard.*"

Tears welled up in Chamberlain's eyes. "It would have made a big difference because I assumed I was pathetic because our life was pathetic."

I answered, "Adults did not say this to you because it was so clear to them that your family situation was not a child's fault and you had no responsibility in it. They assumed you knew what they knew. Unfortunately, they didn't think about this from a child's perspective. They knew it was the responsibility for adults to run your household, but they missed the opportunity to make things better for you by just telling you your situation was a grownup problem."

Chamberlain sighed with relief and repeated, "It would have made a big difference if someone had said to me then what you just said."

CONCLUSION

When kids have erroneous thoughts because they do not understand a situation correctly, guiding them through the three basic steps discussed in this chapter usually helps their thinking. Corrected thinking can change how people feel and behave. In review, the three basic steps to helping young people believe correctly are:

1) Help young people clarify their thoughts and feelings.
2) Validate them.
3) State the truth and who has the power in their circumstances.

After clarifying thoughts and feelings, it is useful to appropriately validate a young person's experience, thoughts and feelings. With validation, kids receive an accurate reflection of their experiences, which leads to internal core development and the ability to trust themselves. Being confident about what one knows and has experienced leads to the development of personal strength - an important attribute for effective living.

Appropriate truth shared with sensitivity can be a turning point for resolution in problems. Truth does not always take away pain, but it generates the opportunity for painful situations to be metabolized, from which young people can emerge with a better understanding of themselves and others. Everyone has to deal with unwanted circumstances like divorces, deaths, moves, illnesses and rejection. Truth within these scenarios enables young people to correctly understand and navigate them, instead of forming erroneous *I am* beliefs and negative strategies that can last a lifetime.

Appropriate truth is also positive information about young people's strengths, potential, skills and abilities, including sensitivities that only those close to them may know. Kids assume that who they are is normal for them. Accurately reflecting back to young people their positive traits enables them to ingest how wise, caring grownups see the good in them, which helps young people find a positive sense of self.

Regarding the issue of power, giving kids an understanding of what they can change and what they cannot change—i.e. where power lies related to problems—enables them to eventually adapt to circumstances beyond their control. Truth may be painful. Yet with truth and the knowledge of where power lies, young people can begin adapting to difficulties without the unnecessary baggage of negative beliefs and self-blame. Appropriate truth is genuinely helpful to children. Positive truth is very useful because it enables kids to build their identities on accurate reflections of themselves, rather than inaccurate assumptions and immature interpretations of life.

These three steps—clarifying, validating, and stating who has the power—are a simple, but useful structure for guiding young people into understanding themselves and the world so they can live within it with the greatest chances for success. When I offer these three elements to adult clients in counseling, they often remark, "I wish I had known this as a kid. It would have made a big difference if I had known then what you are telling me now."

Some of what I have said to adults about their painful childhoods could have been said to them as young people. This would have helped them move beyond their young perspectives, such as the tendency of seeing themselves at the center of circumstances and feeling responsible for situations over which they had no control. In counseling, adults talk about their negative *I am* beliefs, which developed in childhood circumstances. The man who said, "My parents were both alcoholics so I knew I was a piece of crap," was wrong, but no adult in his life ever challenged his way of thinking.

Why not help kids get things right as young people when we have the power to do so?

Chapter Four
More on What Children Believe

There are many complexities to what young people believe. Chapter Three discusses four over-arching principles to understanding children's thoughts, but four principles do not fully encompass how kids perceive, misperceive and make meaning out of their lives. Often young people are not mature or informed enough to understand a situation correctly, sometimes they are directly told misinformation, and kids form their own ways of thinking based on the concrete and subjective aspects of an experience. Occasionally, young people are right and grownups are wrong. This chapter expands on the principles previously discussed and offers additional aspects of thinking about:

- The unconditional love young people have for their parents
- Kids sometimes know what grownups do not know
- Children assume adults have the same information kids have
- Young people become confused by mismatching communication
- Peers can be more important than anything else in a teen's life
- Young family members and divorce
- Children can relate the thoughts and feelings of their births

CHILDREN LOVE THEIR BIOLOGICAL PARENTS

A child's first love is a biological parent. Nothing can take away the love kids have for their biological moms and dads, including parents going to jail or drug treatment, going through divorce, and fighting with partners. Kids are powerless people whose lives depend on the adults who brought them into world.

They innately love their moms and dads and usually have a desire to live with them. In some cases, young people feel embarrassed if they do not live with their biological parents as other kids do. They think about their biological parents very differently than adults who have to remove young people from bad situations in order to keep them safe.

One of the first clients in my clinical practice was a 14-year-old girl named Jaida who had spent the previous decade in foster care. It became clear at the beginning of her treatment that Jaida whole-heartedly wanted to live with her biological mom. The mother had been in prison for half the years my client was in foster care and in drug rehabilitation the other half. As a new therapist, Jaida's thinking did not make sense to me. Her mom was a drug addict who repeatedly put Jaida in unsafe situations and continued to use crack cocaine regardless of the impact on her daughter.

A few decades later, now I know that young people come pre-wired to love their parents, and in most cases, they have an idealized view of how their 'real' moms and dads would care for them. They assume a missing parent would have the unconditional love for them they have for their missing parent. Unfortunately, parents do not always love kids the way kids love their moms and dads and for many reasons youngsters cannot live with their biological parents.

We miss an important viewpoint if we don't take into account how the world seems to young people, and the degree to which they innately long for their biological families. As mentioned, children and pets are the unconditional lovers on our planet. Even when they are neglected, abused and mistreated, most often kids hold a genuine love in their hearts for their real moms and dads. They are naturally dependent on their mothers for care and they can have a mythical love for a parent they have never met. It is important to keep this in mind when we help youngsters through the process of adoption, foster care, and separation. Separating couples usually have some degree of angst against the other partner by the time a partnership ends, but young people do not share the angst in the same way as their parents—kids love, even when they are being hurt, in many cases.

Hardworking caregivers who are filling in for absent or unsafe parents can be discouraged by the unrelenting desire kids have for their biological moms and dads. Grandparents, who step in to care for their grandchildren when natural parents are unable to do so, know the pain of sacrificing themselves for a young person's care and hearing the grandchild's heartbreak and longing for their moms and dads.

Stepparents have the same issue. Faithful, dedicated stepparents can endlessly give of themselves and be better parents than a natural parent, but have to field youngsters' disappointment, longing and unrealistic idealization for their 'real' moms and dads. Children cannot help but seek the love of a biological parent, which often does not make sense to others until they understand that kids come pre-wired to love, and to specifically love the people who gave them birth. Young people can be supported to move beyond this natural longing to some degree, but comments and attempts to reach out to biological parents usually continue into adulthood, often with unsatisfied hopes and yearnings.

Bethany was raising her stepchildren whose mother lived in another state. Bethany said, "The girls (ages five and seven) come home with a drawing from school and say, 'I want to send this to my real mom. Can we mail it to her?'" Bethany said their enthusiasm to show themselves and their work to the most important person in their lives—an idealized birth mother in a different state— was hurtful to her. She was doing the hard work of raising her husband's children, as well as her own, but her stepchildren's loyalty went first to their biological mom.

It might be safe to say that a majority of people wish to be recognized and validated by the people who gave them birth. Adopted kids, after they have been blessed by a birthday party that would never have occurred in the home of a birth parent, may say, "I wish my real mom could be here," and young adults graduating from college or basic military training expose their hearts with comments like, "I wish my parents could have been here to see me graduate," —even if the missing parent is a drug addict or has never been identified. The heart has its reasons, and children are wired to love their parents.

I hear from kids who have been adopted out of severe childhood neglect and abuse that they want to go back and live with their moms and dads even if it means living in a car or a drug environment. Kids who were adopted as babies because their mothers were very young say to adopted parents, "My real mom isn't a teenager anymore. Can I go live with her now?"

To address the innate truth that adopted children love their biological parents, I recommend that caregivers validate, and try not to explain away, a young person's innate love for their natural parents. I say to young clients, "Everybody loves their mom and dad. You can love your birth mom and dad with your whole heart." If it is appropriate I add, "And you can love your adopted mom (or stepmom) too. You have a heart that can love a lot of people and its okay to love more than one mom or dad."

Kids are relieved by this information. They know they love their adoptive moms and dads and they appreciate being given permission to love their birth parents, even if others find the biological parent undesirable.

Adults can minimize a child's natural love for an unsavory parent, which they try to explain with phrases like, "Your dad is just a drug addict and doesn't deserve your love. Forget about him. He's never going to take good care of you anyway."

Phrases like these suggest to young people they are wrong for loving birth parents. Such comments do not deter children from loving their natural parents; instead they train kids to hide their thoughts and internalize potentially harmful beliefs about their own value as the offspring of despicable parents. Kid's identities are affected by negative comments about their birth parents because they see their own identity and worth naturally tied to their human origins.

A better response than to criticize birth parents is to communicate that it's okay to love a natural parent, and there is nothing wrong with them because of their parent's behavior. If we don't tell kids in difficult situations what is true about them, they will draw their own conclusions, which can easily include negative ideas about their own identities. In the mind of an impressionable youngster, a drug-using parent can easily translate into the internalized belief *I'm a bad kid.*

SOMETIMES KIDS KNOW WHAT ADULTS DON'T KNOW

Young people see and hear things adults do not witness, and kids intuitively perceive realities adults miss, because adults are busy handling other matters in life. Children live in their imaginary and spiritual worlds, as well as the concrete world. They start their lives with sensitive hearts and open minds.

Amanda, an adult client, was extremely sensitive as a child, and reported to her parents that she saw her deceased grandmother around their home. Occasionally she told them, "Nana doesn't like this," or "Nana says you shouldn't treat me this way," which was met with parental sarcasm and contempt. I wanted to respect Amanda's perspective, while discovering if she was reporting childhood imagination or if she had actually seen her grandmother. I asked her directly.

Amanda emphatically answered, "I actually saw my grandma! My parents didn't believe me, but I know I saw my Nana. She looked like a real person except shadowy. I think she came to help me because my growing up years were so hard."

I had compassion for the challenges Amanda faced in childhood knowing something a parent would not believe because I, too, had been the adult who could not comprehend what a child was telling me.

When our son David was five years old, my husband and I converted the daylight basement of our home into a mother-in-law apartment and my husband's parents came to live with us. His father was 85 years old and his mother was 82 years old when they moved across the country.

One night at bedtime David said, "I'm afraid Grandma and Grandpa are going to die because they are so old." Just like my client's parents from the previous story, I rebuffed his perspective. A week later, David brought up his concern again at bedtime and I quickly dismissed his idea again. One month later David began to wet the bed. Bed-wetting had not been an issue for him since potty training years earlier, so we were struggling to make sense of this new problem. After a couple of weeks, it became clear that bed-wetting was not going away on its own and I used, for the first time, a technique I often employ in my counseling office.

When we were alone at bedtime, I said to David, "Let's suppose there is a boy, about five or six years old, who did not wet the bed before, but then he started wetting the bed at night. Let's try to figure out what is going on inside him that makes him wet the bed now. Do you have any ideas?"

David earnestly shook his head no—he did not have any ideas.

"Hmmm," I pondered out loud. "Let's take turns guessing and see if we can figure this out. I'll go first. I wonder if the boy is wetting the bed because he has a new sister or his grandma and grandpa moved in." I looked at David to see if this might be the correct answer.

"No, that's not it," he answered confidently.

"Now it's your turn to guess," I said.

"Maybe the boy is afraid of the dark," David offered seriously.

"Is that it?" I checked.

"No, that's not it," he answered.

To make the game fun, I offered something silly. "Maybe he's afraid he is going to turn into something weird, like this puppet," I suggested, while grabbing a beloved character nearby.

"No, that's not going to happen," he replied earnestly. We went back and forth with a few guesses.

Simply because he had said this more than once, not due to any great wisdom or insight, I tried, "Maybe the boy is afraid his grandma and grandpa will die."

With these words, a visible transformation rippled through David's body and his countenance shifted. He morphed in front of my eyes. "That's it," he said with tears.

"Are you worried that grandma and grandpa might die?" I asked with tenderness.

"Yes," he acknowledged.

"Do you think maybe that's why you are wetting the bed?" I inquired with genuine kindness.

"Uh, huh" he softly replied.

Our guessing game helped me understand that the matter about his grandparents' death was a serious topic for him. I switched our conversation and confirmed that older people die. I told him we do not always know when older people will die, but we often have an idea because they may be sick or give us some other indication. I assured him neither of his grandparents were sick and that we did not expect them to die anytime in the near future. Our discussion came to a natural conclusion and we said goodnight with a sweet tenderness between us. David did not wet the bed that night or any nights that followed.

Four weeks later, Grandpa Jim had a stroke during a surgical procedure and died with virtually no warning.

Now I know that David sensed what was happening with his Grandpa when they moved in, which he voiced in an honest, childlike way. As a sensitive child, David intuitively knew something I could not grasp.

Sometimes what children see and hear is intuitive; other times it is very concrete but still unbelievable. A woman in her sixties told me about such a situation. Her son, his wife, and their three-year-old daughter moved in to save money to buy their own home. Three-year-old Tiffany was an early riser. Tiffany and her grandma's partner were often the only ones awake before 6:00 am and Tiffany's parents greatly appreciated that 'Grandpa', which Tiffany called him, was willing to keep track of their child in the mornings while the parents got a few extra minutes of sleep.

One day at breakfast, Tiffany's mother asked her, "What did you and Grandpa do this morning when you were up early?"

"We went to a lady's house," Tiffany sweetly answered.

Tiffany's mother asked a few more questions and discovered that the lady was Grandpa's friend, with whom they had coffee, milk and donuts.

"What did you do after the donuts and milk?" the mother continued, attempting to remain calm so as not to alarm her child, but growing irritated that her mother-in-law's partner felt the freedom to take her child out of the house while they slept.

"We came home," Tiffany answered and attempted to leave.

"Just one more question," her mother said. "Have you gone to the lady's house before?"

"Uh huh," Tiffany sweetly answered with a nod. "A few times… can I go now?"

As it turned out, the child was innocently reporting the woman with whom the grandfather was having an affair. Fortunately, Tiffany was not penalized for naively telling the truth.

Many children are caught between what they know—intuitively or concretely—and what adults will accept from them. It is not uncommon for children to be punished and shamed for innocently speaking the truth when their truth-telling exposes something adults do not want to hear. In Tiffany's case, her grandmother's partner admitted the affair and moved out of the grandmother's house into the other woman's home. The grandmother's family discontinued all contact with the partner, but Tiffany missed the morning adventures with her 'grandfather' and occasionally asked if she could go to the Donut Lady's house and see him.

Tiffany did not receive blame from her grandmother, but many adults blame children for lying when adults do not want to hear what children are saying to them. Kids can be accused of making trouble when they are merely reporting facts. Young people have a need to off-load the weight of something they carry beyond their maturity and they do so in childish ways, which may bring them unfortunate consequences. It is hard to have a child naively blurt out something a family has agreed to ignore. After a young person has brought something difficult into the open, a good solution is to follow the child's lead with appropriate, non-reactive questions to discover what part of the young person's tale is make-believe and what part is truth.

There are many levels of knowing inside family groups. Adults know things kids do not know, kids know things parents do not know and some family members are privy to information withheld from other family members. In addition, like Tiffany's example, children overhear conversations or observe behavior that was not intended for them to see or hear. "Little pitchers have big ears," is a euphemism for kid's capacity to know many things from the adult world, some of which are not appropriate for their age or understanding.

Kids may report what they concretely or intuitively know, but if grownups do not have the frame of reference to make sense of what kids are telling them, adults consider a child's words imaginary or inflated. Youngsters can be very dramatic and creative.

They can fluidly move between reality and make-believe. Yet all kids are placed in situations where they see and hear information that is factual, or they perceive truth in their midst with their many ways of knowing things. When considering the idea that adults won't believe what a child is thinking, we have to realize young people hear and witness many things we don't know they have witnessed. Sometimes kids know what adults don't know.

YOUNG PEOPLE ASSUME ADULTS HAVE THE SAME IN-FORMATION; THEREFORE, KIDS DO NOT SHARE OR VERIFY WHAT THEY HEAR

The following is a benign, long-standing tradition from the Boy Scouts. New troop members are instructed by older scouts and leaders to go from campsite to campsite on their first camping trip to borrow another troop's smoke shifter. The new scouts are also sent out at night to hunt snipes. Experienced Boy Scouts enjoy these traditions because they know there are no snipes or smoke-shifters, truths the Tenderfoots discover in time. Commonly, when given directions to begin a snipe hunt or borrow a smoke shifter, young new scouts do not have the courage to ask, "What is a snipe? What is a smoke-shifter?" because they might be embarrassed by not knowing what other scouts know. These traditions continue in fun as new scouts naively hunt for snipes and seek out smoke-shifters.

Because kids are young and learn new information regularly, young people do not always check one adult's word against another or verify what they hear from peers and siblings. Reasons for this include: they do not want to seem naïve, they do not want to verify information they dislike, or like the Tenderfoots, they are simply too young and inexperienced to know they should get corroborating information.

Alcoholic and other dysfunctional families operate with the unspoken rules of *don't talk, don't trust, don't feel*. No one has to explain these strategies to young people in their families—they adopt these coping mechanisms for survival and learn them by observing other family members. In many cases, kids assume adults already know what kids know, which is not always the case.

Tiffany naively shared her adventures to the Donut Lady's house because no one prompted her to remain silent. Nor did an adult think how natural it would be for Tiffany to blurt out where she had been because children usually assume what they know, everyone knows. Often, young people are not sophisticated enough to decipher what they should and should not tell to others.

Young people's naiveté can keep them from sharing about one adult's behavior to another because they accept what happens to them as normal. Young children in daycare usually do not report abuse because they accept the behavior of adults and presume their parents know about what is happening in the settings where they spend their days. Kids assume their parents are aware of what takes place when the babysitter, relative or close friend babysits them or takes them on special outings. Even though a perpetrator's behavior is disturbing to kids, not all young people spontaneously report what is happening because they assume their caregivers already know or they fear punishment for telling.

I have asked more than one adult client seeking therapy for childhood sexual abuse if they told their caregivers what was happening at the time. The majority of clients have said, "No," followed by, "I assumed they knew because they let me go on outings with our family friend;" "I was afraid they wouldn't do anything about it and I had to accept what was happening;" "I was too ashamed to tell," or, "I was trained to obey adults and I was supposed to obey the daycare lady."

I have not met a single adult who was sexually molested as a child who wanted the sexualized behavior yet most did not tell the adults what was happening because they made inaccurate assumptions. This concept applies to other family issues as well.

Young people in divorced families know there will be conflict if they report certain aspects of one parent's behavior to the other parent. Out of self-preservation, kids withhold information to minimize conflict between their caregivers. Kids are afraid there will be ramifications for them if they tell an adult what is happening, or they assume adults already know. Obviously, these assumptions are not always correct.

Ideally, caregivers will be proactive and create environments which encourage kids to talk about situations that challenge them. Young people can be prepared for situations they might encounter without scaring them. Kids of all ages generally understand the concept of rules. They can be told there is a rule that no one is supposed to touch them where their swimming suit goes and if someone wants to touch them there they should tell a trusted adult. Giving simple instructions and simple truths is a proactive way adults can circumvent young peoples' natural inclination to assume all the adults in their lives have the same knowledge or perspectives kids have.

CHILDREN BECOME CONFUSED BY NON-VERBAL COMMUNICATION THAT DOES NOT MATCH VERBAL COMMUNICATION

The first book a child ever reads is the book of a caregiver's emotions and body language. Babies scan their caretaker's faces for emotional, non-verbal cues. When a stranger approaches, even very young infants focus attention on their mother's faces, reading her reaction. Children learn to read visual cues and their parents' emotional energy first and later develop the capacity to understand verbal communication. Body language, emotions and words are the communication channels people decipher in order to engage in meaningful communication. Kids tend to take verbal communication at face value and become confused when non-verbal data—the first channel of communication—does not match verbal messages.

For very young children through adolescence, it is almost impossible to process words, emotions and body signals that do not match one another. With maturity, people develop the capacity to interpret and respond to information in such a way that they can override mismatching data in healthy ways, but kids are confused when words, body signals and intuitive data don't match. When this happens, kids often attribute something negative about themselves to explain their lack of understanding.

An example of mismatching data is a caregiver who is clearly angry, but says to a youngster, "I'm not mad." In such a case, the young person knows through body-sensing that the adult is angry. The young person uses an immature mind to assume the caregiver is angry with them because no other reasons are evident. Without additional information, naturally self-centric young people fill in

99

the gaps between what they experience and what they hear by concluding something is wrong with themselves.

An alternative to sending mixed messages to kids regarding an adult's mood or reaction is for the adult to briefly state what is true, followed by a simple explanation within the young person's level of understanding. An example is, "You can probably tell I'm upset, but I'm not upset with you. I found out today that our car needs some very expensive repairs." Adding another phrase which relates to the child's perspective is also very helpful, such as, "I'm worried about having enough money, but this is a grownup problem and I'll use my grownup brain to figure something out. Things always work out."

Stating what a parent knows and taking responsibility for it sidesteps a young person's inclination to process what happens in their environment to be about themselves. It avoids the potential for kids to seek ways to solve adult problems. Family equilibrium depends on the stability of adults. Without equilibrium, young people compensate for emotional instability with young and un-informed tools to keep their home environments in balance.

As mentioned, people receive data from their environments with all three of their brains—cranium, heart and gut. Knowing that kids become confused when verbal, emotional and intuitive information does not match, adults can help them learn to inter-pret data accurately. If adults don't intercept their meaning-mak-ing process, youngsters will invariably come up with interpreta-tions of their own, which often infer something negative about themselves.

JOINING WITH PEERS CAN BE MORE IMPORTANT THAN ANYTHING ELSE IN A TEENAGER'S WORLD

Humans are innately designed to have connections with other humans and teenagers are in the process of moving out of their home-based dependence toward more social dependence on their peer groups. Young people in this phase seek independence from their parents and greater connection with people outside their family circles. This is the natural process of life that moves ado-lescents toward adulthood.

Getting Out of a Parent's Gravity is my name for this outward movement. The title represents the effort and energy it takes to blast off from a natural, grounding environment such as the earth's gravity or parental attachment, into a new stratosphere less tethered to the foundational source. Space shuttles require a great a deal of energy to initially propel them out of earth's gravitational field. Adolescents are the same—they are gathering their internal resources and sense of self in preparation for launching into a larger world. The initial, most important destination for a teenager's launch is the adolescent peer group—other young adults who are emerging from their homes. Together they form a new strata of society. Successfully getting into the new strata is as important for adolescents as it is for a space shuttle to successfully break out of the earth's gravitational pull.

Since the developmental task of adolescence is to move from one social system to another, teenagers are in a heightened peer-connection process. Their innate developmental process means that peers, not parents, are more highly esteemed for social norms and values—albeit immature ones.

Most adolescents have insecurities about themselves as burgeoning members of their new world, and they use their expanding environments to determine their sense of value. Unfortunately, undervaluing the self, in comparison to others, can be a natural outcome for young people who are attempting to differentiate from caregivers and establish themselves as individuals in a new social order. Other insecure teenagers are not the best reflection of a teen's true identity yet it is in this unstable new milieu that young people begin to establish their own ways of thinking and patterns of living.

Parents cannot prevent teens from wanting greater connection to their peers yet not all attempts to launch and join the emerging social order turn out well. As part of social connectivity, people instinctively order themselves into complex social tiers. Elaine Aron, in her book *The Undervalued Self,* refers to human social organization as the same innate ranking process as a canine pack. She speaks to the depression that follows when attempts at social connection are unsuccessful.

Depression is not uncommon in adolescence. Parents observe their teens striving for connection and participation, but also withdrawing from the emotional injuries that inevitably occur as young people attempt to join new social orders. Success or failure at joining can lead to long-lasting self-evaluation about a teen's identity and personal value. These judgments by self or others can contribute to low self-esteem and develop into strategies to offset the pain of failed connections to the peer group. Strategies can include drug use and other temporary methods for self-soothing. Such strategies and *I am* beliefs have the potential to last a lifetime.

Adults can underestimate the impact of a teen's success and failure in attempting to join their peer groups. I suggest caregivers talk with teenagers about the process they are going through and normalize that all kids feel the way they feel sometimes. Teens can give parents the impression that nothing their parents say matters to them, but actually the opposite is true. Evidence supports that parents, even though seemingly ignored, are the most influential presence in a teen's life. Understanding and supporting teenagers in their innate drive to join a social structure greater than their family of origin is important. Adults initiating conversation with a young person is key to helping them in this process. Not all teens will begin talking about how it is going for them in their attempts to join social circles, but virtually all teens care about this subject. When parents extend subtle or overt invitations for discussions about life with friends outside the family, they are communicating knowledge and respect that this is one of the most important aspects of a teenager's life.

The four common ways young people think about themselves is heightened during adolescence and shaped by the feedback loop of social interactions. As a reminder, they are:

1. Young people perceive themselves at the center and use cause-and-effect thinking to understand their worlds. Even as teens, they can erroneously believe *I caused it* because success or failure at joining a new social order seems very concrete and personal to young people seeking to belong.

2. Young people take words at face value. Praise, criticism, words said in jest, hurtful, angry outbursts and more turn into *I believe it.* Taking as truth the comments from other insecure adolescents is a skewed frame of reference.

3. Young people convert experiences into defining information about themselves, which translates into positive and negative *I am*...beliefs. Since peers are more important than parents in many cases at this developmental stage, the defining statements teens hear from other immature minds carry tremendous weight. As teens are attempting to establish their worth, they are at risk to find themselves deficient because the reflective lens they are using is quite unstable.

4. Positive and negative experiences in life can lead to long-standing strategies, which means *I adapt to it.* Adolescents adjust to their exciting and unstable peer environments with new and riskier strategies. They have the bodies of adults and the emotional maturity of teenagers, which lead them to experiment and develop values and new behaviors of their own.

In summary, adolescents are using the fairly unstable world of teen life as a context for the four thought processes above. They develop patterns for living out of the cauldron of teen life, which means their beliefs and behaviors can get off course due to youth and inexperience. The innate inclination to perceive peers as more important than parents means these four developmental issues are being shaped by potentially inaccurate sources. Inaccurate or not, the success or failure at joining the social peer group and these resultant four ways of thinking, can be powerful determinants in how young people chart the remainder of their lives.

A solution I recommend for this teenage evolution is for adults to continue inputting correct and positive data into adolescent's lives, even if teens appear to not be listening. This subject is further developed in the *Perspectives* section of this book.

CHILDREN AND DIVORCE

Stephanie, a 40-year-old client, was bereft when her father died because it meant there was no remaining possibility that her parents would get back together after their divorce. She had spent three decades hoping her parents would reunite, which would mean she would no longer be the offspring of separated parents. Her father's passing was the death of a dream. Stephanie's situation might be extreme, but young people can miscomprehend the finality of their parents' divorce and remain hopeful for their parents to get back together.

Divorce may start a process of relief for conflicted adults, but it can be the beginning of very difficult changes for youngsters in a family. Even though they have heard their parents argue and experienced the collateral damage of their parents' conflict, divorce is generally interpreted by young people in terms of what it means for them. Divorce may bring financial hardship, less stability, more responsibility and increased isolation. It is generally inconvenient to live in two households and get along with step families. From a young person's perspective, apart from having their parents stop fighting, divorce is only good news for kids if it makes their lives better. Youngsters can adapt to divorce and there are strategies which help kids adapt to divorce more effectively than others. Learning how young people understand their situations and their sense of self in relation to divorce is one of the highest priorities for helping them navigate through it.

The four basic thought processes of youngsters—*I caused it, I believe it, I am* beliefs, and *I adapt to it*—apply to young people and divorce. Depending on their ages, kids may inaccurately construe something they have done as part of the reason for the divorce (*I caused it*). They may internalize the divorce or words about others as meaning about themselves, including hurtful remarks about the other parent (*I believe it*). Divorce can influence the identities of kids (*I am...* beliefs) and young people develop ways to cope with their changing circumstances (*I adapt to it*). These internalized beliefs can become long-standing patterns.

Each of these points is evident in the story of Anna, an adopted child whose parents divorced. Anna's mother initially brought four-year-old Anna to counseling before the divorce because she

104

showed signs of attachment problems from her years in an orphanage. The mother was an attuned, loving parent and dedicated herself to helping the young girl adjust to their family. Anna became very dependent on her mother. Two years after her adoption, Anna's parents divorced and the court ordered equal time between the two parental households despite professional evidence that suggested Anna was struggling with stable attachment. In one of our counseling sessions, the mother said Anna was inconsolable when she had to be physically extracted from her arms by the father and taken to his house for several days. In light of the four points regarding kids' thinking, I suggested she tell Anna that Anna had done nothing wrong to make her go to her daddy's house and that she was still a very good girl.

The mother looked puzzled trying to understand how these comments would be useful in a situation that was not caused by Anna or related to her daughter's worth. Yet at the next parking lot transfer when Anna was inconsolable and begging not to go to Daddy's, the mother said to Anna, "You did not do anything wrong to make this happen and you are still a very good girl."

Anna's crying decreased at once because she took her mother's words at face value. Anna's mother spoke to the difficult situation from the child's perspective with truth. Anna's young cause-and-effective thinking led her to believe that what was happening to her was caused by her and it meant she was bad. Anna was distraught about an *I am* belief she formulated about herself. When her mother corrected Anna's inaccurate conclusions, Anna's response changed. Anna developed strategies to cope with her situation, but not all of her strategies were helpful. One of her coping mechanisms was to switch loyalty at her father's house and punish her mother by saying, "I hate you and I want to stay at Daddy's house." Her mother wisely responded with kindness and said, "I love you wherever you are." In response, Anna broke down crying and said, "I want to come home."

Kid's strategies to deal with the impact of divorce can include over-functioning to help a parent, under-functioning due to stress, acting out behaviors, decreased performance in school and others. Parents sometimes begin to use their children as sounding boards or messengers between them, which creates unnecessary strain on kids trying to find their own way through the destabilization of their families. Divorce requires youngsters to make some adaptation to the changing family unit, which can be positive, negative or a combination of both. Strategies that emerge for kids during divorce can be role changes like stepping up to be the 'man of the house' when they are 10 to 20 years old, raising younger siblings, or making as few demands as possible. These, and many others, are the strategies young people develop to cope with changes that come with the breakup of their families. Kids in life, and specifically in major life changes like divorce, need as much stability as possible, and many of the strategies they develop are directly correlated to finding balance within their unraveling family systems.

Michelle Beaudreau, a school counselor for children ages 12 through 18 years old, reports the level of stability divorcing parents provided for their children was the single most important factor in determining how well kids continued to perform in school during their parents' divorce. Beaudreau observed that youngsters maintained emotional and academic performance at school if their parents continued to provide reliable structure and boundaries during separation, but if structure and boundaries fell away in the divorce process, kid's success at school followed the same trajectory. The school staff saw a bell curve of instability during family dissolution for each student in divorcing families unless parents worked to maintain structure and continuity for their children.

Young people's self-identities can be impacted by challenging circumstances. Kids usually compare themselves to others and divorce is a circumstance which becomes part of their comparison, reflecting something about themselves—most of which is self-supposed and not confirmed by others. Divorce can be a heightened situation where young people define themselves by the emotions, behaviors and words of others. The best way for caregivers to mitigate erroneous beliefs and perceptions is to assure kids that the divorce is not their fault and they are still good people in spite of the family's dissolution. This reassurance incubates, even if a cavalier teen replies, "Whatever..."

Intentionally inserting truth for kids is not always easy for emotionally strained parents and youngsters do not always give the impression that parental support is helpful. But words linger and make a difference for young people who are trying to find their own identities in the midst of divorce. Intentional, appropriate truth increases a child's chances for coming through a divorce with right thinking about themselves and others.

CHILDREN FORM BELIFS FROM THEIR BIRTHS, WHICH BECOME A TEMPLATE FOR LIFE

The body holds memory, including the memory of birth. As previously discussed, the body processes and remembers on several levels, including consciously and unconsciously. It may seem unlikely that the mind and body hold the complete memory of birth, but I observe children who quite readily reveal how they came to think about themselves and their safety in the world during the birth process. Over the decades, I have noticed that the struggle which brings clients to counseling often contains elements of their birth story in it.

For example, it is not uncommon for clients who were stuck in the birth canal to find themselves stuck in life and unable to move from one stage of life to the next. Remarkably, when I use Lifespan Integration with clients to help them heal their birth experiences, they can generally relate a sense of what was happening to them during their births. I do not use hypnosis or any other form of unconscious access to do this; I just give them the opportunity to share what is happening emotionally and psychologically as part of the LI process.

The parents of a 17-year-old came to my office seeking help for their son who they described as having a hard time moving forward. They asked to meet alone with me for the first session, in which they explained that throughout life their son often had to be pushed to enter new situations and he procrastinated in circumstances where he needed to take action like filling out college applications. He resisted their efforts to motivate him toward initiative and self-activation. The parents sought counseling for their son because they were concerned about his readiness to leave home for college within the next few months. I asked about his birth.

His parents told me the mother was seven and half months pregnant when she developed a serious illness, which hospitalized her. Doctors made the decision to deliver their son six weeks prematurely to protect the mother's health.

"How did it go?" I asked.

"Not very well," the mother answered. "The doctor intervened to start labor, but the baby moved very slowly through the birth canal. After many hours of labor, the doctor used forceps to deliver the baby. It took a while, but eventually the doctor got him out of there."

"Would 'stuck' generally describe your son?" I asked.

The parents looked at each other. They answered, "To some degree, yes, but he's also really smart. He succeeds at school and other things when we get him started."

I replied, "Being successful and being stuck are two different things. Your son may be reflecting some degree of birth trauma in his life. We will address his birth experience as part of our counseling."

When I met with their son for counseling, I learned that many aspects of his life reflected his birth experience. He told me he very often felt afraid to enter new experiences because he did not feel ready.

"Not quite developed enough?" I asked.

"Yes, something like that," he said, "like I'm not quite old enough yet, even though I am the same age as my classmates."

The young man explained that his parents often forced him to enter new experiences of their choosing and he was unsuccessful resisting their efforts. He was an angry teenager who had been quite controlled. His birth experience appeared to be a template that played out repeatedly in his life. With regularity, he seemed not quite ready for the events of life and very resistant to outside pressure.

All children and most adults have been able to describe a sense of their birth experiences when I worked with them. One three-year-old, whose mother had a probe inserted through her belly during labor, spontaneously mentioned that his baby-self's head had a poke in it. "Ouch! I got a poke," he said.

Each time we went through the story of his birth, the young client spontaneously reached up and touched the place on his head where the probe entered. His mother confirmed that the probe inserted through her belly did pierce the infant's head in the exact place he was touching and that she had not told him about the probe. The young client stopped touching his head where the poke took place after his mind and body understood the challenges of his birth were over.

I have come to believe a young person's innate personality is reflected as early as birth, and the birth experience is reflected in how they express their innate personalities throughout life. Birth becomes part of a child's thinking and reflects in their behavior. Traumatic births are powerful experiences that deeply impress the body to guard against danger into a newborn's psyche. I believe some children are born with PTSD, which is a concept that is further developed in the following chapter.

Chapter Five
What Children Learn from Trauma

A form of conditioned learning occurs in traumatic situations. During a trauma, the limbic system takes over and activates responses about safety within the human brain. Within the limbic system is the amygdala—the brain's fear center—which activates when the external world sends hints of real or perceived threats.

Doctors delivering a child who is having trouble moving through the birth canal know they have many options for monitoring and assuring that birth goes well, but the infant who is experiencing the difficulty does not know these resources are available and will be provided as needed. Infants feel trapped, anxious, and hopeless when they cannot resolve their situations and some of this first occurs for them during birth. Their bodies remember the experiences and respond to future events from a brain system which has learned very early in life that danger is present and personally unresolvable. Information learned through a trauma gets top priority when circumstances later in life hint at the thoughts and feelings of the original traumatizing event.

In addition to the limbic system activating in a trauma, the front and mid parts of the brain may go offline so the body can react without overthinking. The front and mid parts of the brain help people decide day-to-day concerns like which cereal to have for breakfast, but they are not the top decision makers needed for quick reactions in potentially life-threatening situations. After danger has passed, these parts of the brain come back on line to take over daily decision-making.

A trauma experience loads memories into the body-mind, which become part of a database for the brain to use for the remainder of life. Sights, smells, sounds and any other reminders of previous traumas can activate the limbic system and cause the body to prepare for danger, even if no danger is currently present. The brain prepares for danger because danger signals are present, but it does not completely shut down the front and mid-brains because a threat is merely perceived—the final call to action has not been sounded. This combination of brain activity leaves individuals with heightened attention, increased heart rate, perspiration, anxiety and other fight or flight symptoms in circumstances where the individual may not actually be in danger. For example, in seemingly benign conditions like spending the night at a trusted friend's house with other kids, a young person may be required to interact socially, remember information, and manage their emotions, while feeling anxious due to the brain's warning system in a non-dangerous environment. This anxiety activates quickly and presents itself in or out of the proper context due to earlier memories.

An example of the brain's out-of-context warning system is from teenager Amanda who had a very serious car crash on a bridge and saw her life flash before her as she approached the bridge railings. Amanda anticipated crashing through the barrier and falling to her death. Instead, the car stopped against the railing and did not go over, but Amanda's brain accurately perceived the incident as potentially life-threatening. Like other traumatized individuals, Amanda's front and mid-brain went dark during the incident, but stayed online when she approached bridges after the bridge scare, which meant her body sent her intense warning signals each time she encountered a bridge. Amanda came to counseling to get over her fear of bridges, which was ruining her driving experience. After her crash, Amanda always felt anxious and afraid when crossing bridges, even though no imminent danger was present. Amanda's story is normal for trauma.

Young people of all ages have these same double-bind circumstances due to traumas, many of which are not recognized as limbic-activating situations that cause stress and anxiety in their bodies.

One such condition is the PTSD which can occur for babies during their births.

SOME CHILDREN ARE BORN WITH PTSD

There are common traumas children experience in their young lives, but one seldom mentioned is the PTSD that occurs for some babies as they are entering the world beyond the womb. These traumas can include the death of a twin in the womb, premature births, incubator stays, periods of oxygen deprivation or surgeries. All these difficulties are remembered by the body and warn individuals to defend against them later.

As mentioned, birth experiences can be a template for life, and traumatic births include common PTSD symptoms within the template. The bodies of babies remember their experiences just like any other PTSD event, after which symptoms of hypervigilance, exaggerated startle reflex, feelings of fear in safe conditions and other trauma markers are present in their young lives. Babies cannot tell us at the time of their births how they experienced trauma, but their bodies know and the limbic system works to keep them safe well beyond the moments of difficult delivery, just like Amanda's body warned her of bridges after her life-threatening crash. Unexplained anxiety, hypervigilance, frightening dreams and exaggerated startle reflex are childhood symptoms that may indicate birth trauma.

Because trauma teaches the body to be hyper alert, kids can become irrationally emotional, over-controlling, or withdrawn because they were helpless to protect themselves at a traumatic point in their lives. They fall back into an emotional, controlling or helpless place when they get conscious or unconscious triggers from their traumas. These types of behavior do not always mean trauma, but for children, trauma generally means some form of these behaviors.

When kids are traumatized they also become anxious. When I encounter anxious kids in my office, I inquire about their births and any other traumas the young person may have experienced. If not treated, their anxiety will prevail into adulthood and not be easily explained or managed.

Trauma leaves kids with erroneous negative beliefs about themselves and conditions them to live in a defensive mode. The simple, cause-and-effect thinking of young people often leads them to believe they caused a trauma to happen and they are bad because of it. The learning that occurs through trauma is not forgotten, but it can be healed. Difficult symptoms are a signal to caregivers to wonder if a trauma has impacted a child's heart, mind, and body.

Kitty's Story

I have worked with many children who meet the criteria for PTSD from their births. They present with anxious symptoms and have a hard time entering into new experiences. Seven-year-old Kitty had unexplained meltdowns, which her mother could not soothe. No amount of holding, calming, or distracting would enable Kitty to down-regulate her emotions. The family brought her to my office because they were being impacted by her emotional dysregulation. Kitty's mother was hoping some form of therapy would help Kitty so she could travel, have play dates and attend birthday parties without high levels of distress. The start of a new school year was torture for her.

I asked the mother about Kitty's birth who explained she was in labor for approximately twenty hours. After a long labor, Kitty had fully descended into the birth canal, but was not proceeding as expected. Doctors let the mother continue in her desire to have a natural birth. Eventually, the baby's monitor indicated extreme distress and they opted for an emergency caesarean section. Kitty was quite unresponsive when she was born and her breathing was very shallow. The medical team revived her. A few days after the birth, Kitty and her mother went home from the hospital, and the doctors said Kitty was a perfectly normal baby – *in every way they could observe.*

I was glad to hear Kitty was physically healthy and normal. She passed through developmental stages as expected. Everything was normal about Kitty except her meltdowns, which were not merely temper tantrums. Apart from knowing her child was always anxious in new situations, the mother could not find any pattern associated with the meltdowns.

I asked Kitty to imagine her birth experience. Using the steps of Lifespan Integration, I took Kitty through each step of the birth story as I knew it, and I asked her to imagine what it was like to be the little baby who was doing everything right to be born, but got stuck. Then I asked her to imagine how the doctors reached in and lifted her out of her mommy, and how they helped her start breathing. She nodded after each part of the story. I took her through a timeline of her life up to her present age of seven years old. We repeated this sequence three times in our first session and three times in a follow-up session. During the second session, when Kitty appeared to be quite connected to the feelings of distress in the birth story, I asked her, "Was your baby-self scared?"

Kitty nodded her head in a solemn, frightened yes.

"Did you think you would die?" I asked, gently.

She sadly nodded yes again.

"But we know the baby lived, right? I asked.

With an enthusiastic smile, she nodded yes one more time and I guided Kitty through repetitions of her Lifespan Integration timeline.

Kitty's mother brought her in for a final, third session, and reported that the meltdowns had virtually ceased. The mother said she could parent Kitty like she did her other children—with love, patience, but also firmness—and Kitty was able to respond appropriately. The mother said, "We knew Kitty was never trying to be difficult, but we couldn't understand what was happening and she couldn't seem to stop it. Now Kitty can follow my instructions and if she is really upset she can tell me what's bothering her. Kitty has never been able to tell us what her crying spells were about."

I did not see Kitty after the third session. Six months later her mother reported that Kitty behaved like a normal seven-year-old girl and no longer had meltdowns. Two years later, the mother sent an email expressing her gratitude for the help Kitty received in my office. The mother said Kitty did not have another meltdown after we met together. She was able to go to birthday parties, spend the night with friends, and the start of the school year made her no more nervous than it did other children. Kitty was able to enter into new experiences and they were able to travel as a family.

Even though this young client could not report the trauma she experienced at birth, Kitty's body held the memory of it, and her limbic system warned her whenever situations reminded her of the trauma. Understandably, her system responded by sending out alerts that were not needed in safe contexts. Kitty was able to have a safe and normal life once her body understood that the birth experience was permanently behind her.

LARGE AND SMALL TRAUMAS

Any trauma a child experiences will load information into the brain and body to be considered for the rest of life. In some psychological circles, these are referred to as big T traumas and little t traumas - defining them as major, life impacting events or small, less impactful traumas, but trauma, nevertheless.

The big T traumas are generally obvious to caregivers. Big T traumas include serious accidents, impactful major life changes, natural disasters, dangerous frightening situations, and other major-scale occurrences. We recognize big T traumas because they change the internal world of almost anyone who experiences them. For example, soldiers in war are exposed to big T trauma. We generally accept that war has had some impact on these men and women, and we know the body has loaded some kind of adjustment mechanism into their minds as a way to deal with the unimaginable. As discussed, once experienced, the adjustment mechanism continues to operate via the limbic system even when people are in safe circumstances. The sense of self is impacted through major trauma, and a person who has experienced a big T trauma will have an aspect of self that holds onto the belief *I am not safe in the world.*

Individuals who experienced the events of 9/11 firsthand report feeling unsafe long after the danger was over. Becky, one of my clients, was present on September 11, 2001 when terrorists attacked the World Trade Center in New York City. Becky was exiting the subway underneath the World Trade Center when she encountered people running for their lives. Becky followed them outdoors and saw an airplane fly into the second of the twin towers.

Becky tried to work at her normal job in Manhattan, but she was very anxious and unable to concentrate. Eventually, Becky left her job, broke off a long-term relationship and moved across the country where she attempted to work again. Even though five years passed, Becky became very frightened when she saw airplanes in the sky and she struggled to concentrate at work. Outsiders might assume that five years after the trauma Becky's body would naturally heal itself and move onto the next phase of life. Unfortunately, that is not how trauma operates in the body. Even though some of Becky's symptoms decreased over time, her body's hyper-vigilance about safety remained.

We were able to heal Becky's PTSD. Her story is an example of what the body comes to believe through a big T trauma. As mentioned, once learned, the body does not easily forget the need to protect itself after danger.

Small *t* traumas are not as easily recognized. An event can happen for a child that a parent assumes is insignificant yet it becomes somewhat traumatic for the child. Seldom will the young person report the event as traumatic, but the learning derived from the experience will operate in the way big T traumas operate—conscious and unconscious reminders will tell the youngster to be on guard. Caregivers may observe young people being afraid and holding back when they should enter into an experience. If this is a change, the behavior might represent a small t trauma, which has not been perceived by outsiders. As mentioned, young brains often load information incorrectly, and events that seem inconsequential to adults can be very troubling for youngsters.

An example of small t trauma includes hearing about something very bad from other kids and not having the context or understanding to process the information. Young people often give each other erroneous ideas without adults knowing this has happened. The loss of a pet can be more impactful to kids than parents might assume and be considered a small t trauma for some. Small traumas are usually indicated by increased emotionality and recurring changes in behavior. Examining the timeframe for a behavioral change and investigating how the young person interpreted events within it, are keys to helping identify and resolve small t traumas. Methods for helping young people identify their small traumas and resulting beliefs are provided in the next section.

RELATIONAL TRAUMA

The most common childhood traumas, according to Los Angeles psychologist Robin L. Kay, Ph.D., are ruptures of a significant emotional attachment. Connection to significant others is required for survival in the human species. Our caveman ancestors stayed alive by functioning within rudimentary societies. Humans are innately tribal, therefore, belonging to a tribe is an aspect of survival, which means the threat-sensitive limbic brain responds to the issues of attachment as matters of life and death.

Joseph's anxiety story, which opened this book, presented as a fear of vomiting at school, but was actually an attachment rupture with his father. The turning point in his therapy came when Joseph said, "That's when I knew I couldn't trust my dad anymore." In Joseph's case, his father had wrongly predicted Joseph would not vomit during the night. After Joseph threw up in his bed, which meant his father was wrong, Joseph lost faith that his personal well-being was in the care of his tribe, specifically as it related to his dad.

Relationship ruptures are behind many trauma responses that activate on their own due to the limbic system's quick response to real or perceived threat. Hints of exile from the tribe, including disapproval and the possibility of rejection, trigger automatic defenses. Adults can underestimate the impact of normal teenage drama for young people because adults have already lived through the challenges of adolescence. The social and relational drama that occurs for teens may seem to adults like normal growing pains, but in reality, they may be experienced as life-changing relationship ruptures for adolescents.

Domination by others, experienced as bullying and social exclusion, have long-term consequences for the brains of young people. Bullying and exclusion can fall into the category of safety and survival within the tribe—at least to the limbic system. Confident teenagers may address social challenges with strength and perseverance, others may cling to one or two friends to navigate the insecure years, and still other teens may withdraw and set a negative course that impacts their lives for years to come. How the brain perceives the dangers of the world, including the matter of belonging, affects how the brain stores the issues of inclusion and safety.

Belonging—a form of connection—is so important to human society that relationship ruptures can occur in settings adults may not perceive as traumatic for kids, such as a foster child leaving the home, the death of a family member, and other 'normal' relationship separations. Unless circumstances are explained in an age-appropriate way, kids can interpret separations inaccurately or with an emotional intensity that causes events to become significant relational ruptures. For example, the adoption of children from orphanages is considered a positive event in many cases, but for the child, adoption may represent significant attachment loss to important caregivers. Situations like these may be trauma for kids, accompanied by unexplainable trauma symptoms, and be misunderstood by adults.

The way to discern if an experience has become traumatic is to find out how young people interpret their experiences and what they believe about themselves as a result. Most adolescents are insecure to some degree, but adolescence is not traumatic for all teenagers. If a change is noted in a young person, it is worth finding out what has happened to create the change, and offering conversations, support and therapy if needed.

Explaining and interpreting a relationship rupture for kids, without negative judgment against them, creates an opportunity for repair. A relationship repair can be accomplished by anyone close to a young person and does not have to include an action from the injuring party. It includes explaining what happened in a manner appropriate to the age of the child, understanding from the youngster's perspective, and helpful, appropriate truth. Fogel writes, "…a parent, an older sibling, a neighbor, or someone else close to a child can repair a rupture in real time, soon after the event, by helping the child to process the reality of the event and the emotions associated with it…The fewer times someone helps you to repair traumas when you're a child, the more negative programming you have as an adult."

We can mitigate the effect of traumas for children by understanding how they internalized their experiences. Larger traumas may need the help of a professional counselor who specializes in helping young people overcome trauma's effects. In other situations, we can help kids resolve trauma and emotional conflicts by giving them appropriate, honest information about their situations, helping them understand the role they played in the problem, and providing positive views about their identities in spite of the circumstance. When we take time to understand a situation from the perspective of concrete young thinkers, we can wisely offer them ways to understand their situations and lighten their loads.

Without intentionally supporting kids to understand themselves in the world correctly, young people will operate out of their own young schemas, which are built on immature thinking. A Swedish proverb says worry gives a small thing a big shadow. Fear, anxiety, and worry stem from feelings of vulnerability and are magnified by loss of faith and hope in the future. Young people can be worried about events large and small. Many times, kids have experienced traumas and relational ruptures which adults do not recognize as impactful. Yet these various-sized traumas can impact kids for years to come.

Making an attempt to understand what kids are thinking and feeling gives them a chance to reset how they have to come to understand themselves and the world.

In review, trauma comes in many sizes and many forms. There are Big T and little t traumas as well as physical, emotional, and relational traumas that may only perceived as traumatic by the one who experienced them.

Chapter Six

The Science of Believing

How do kids come to believe what they believe? Not simply through will or effort in most cases, as mentioned. Learning—the process of taking in data, storing it and using it later—occurs on many levels and includes many factors. Young people of different ages have different levels of brain wave activity, which affects what they learn at each stage, and humans have more than one brain as informational processing centers. The same type of nerve cell that fires in the cranium is also densely clustered in the gut and heart area. Each of these regions can be considered a brain dedicated to receiving and processing different forms of data. Youngsters' ways of thinking are influenced by their environments, which their cells cannot help but absorb. In addition, kids learn through conditioning, which raises the question of nature versus nurture. Are young people a product of their environments or are they merely fulfilling innate tendencies? Each of these scientific ideas is briefly presented as an underpinning to how young people come to believe as they do.

The metaphor of geological strata is useful in understanding the nature of internal belief systems. Fire, drought, the death of a tree, or the drying of an ocean can be seen in the geological layers along a roadway. The layers may be thick, dark, narrow, rocky, or red in one layer and grey in the next, depending on the events and conditions present when the soil layers were deposited. The layers indicate that what happened on that piece of earth was loaded there and remains many years later. Geological strata are analogous to the process that deposits information into the neural networks of humans—what happens around people ends up inside

121

them. The human mind is comprised of complex layering, which includes beliefs, emotions and experiences held within the body. Thoughts, feelings, behaviors, and events long past contribute to ongoing neural firing patterns.

Knowledge about the mind is expanding at a vast rate and the following resources briefly give insight into the complex function and interconnection of the human brain. A few summary ideas are presented here as an elementary introduction into the science behind young peoples' thinking.

BRAIN WAVES

Brain wave levels contribute to how young people think about themselves and their environments. Kids think the ways they do because their brain wave frequencies are correlated to their state of childhood, which change as kids develop. Babies sleep a lot, young children love imagination, and teenagers achieve complex learning due to increasing brain wave cycles. Therefore, youngsters cannot be expected to think like adults when they do not have mature brain operating systems. A brief summary of the progressive brain wave patterns follows.

Babies are most often in the slowest brain wave frequency of .5 to 4 cycles per second, which is why they generally spend a majority of their time sleeping. This cycle is identified as delta.

Children ages two through six spend their waking hours in the next level of brain activity identified as theta, with 4-8 cycles per second. This level of brain speed is associated with hypnosis and is the state in which humans are the most open to suggestion. In this highly programmable state, information can be directly downloaded into the human mind. Two-through six-year-olds record vast amounts of information during this stage, yet they do not have the capacity to evaluate or choose which information becomes absorbed into their young minds. The positive outcome for this brain speed is that by age six youngsters have picked up language, sleep patterns, relationship styles and behaviors acceptable to their cultures without filter. The bad news about this imaginative, open state is that negative thoughts, feelings and experiences present in their environments also become the internal states of young children and influence them to their very cells.

These early absorbed states sit in the unconscious brain and act as a resource for the rest of life. Early information stored in the unconscious mind does not go away over time. Even though a child matures and develops new perspectives, the unconscious brain uses its whole cache of information to navigate the world. The unconscious brain can easily override the conscious brain.

Children ages 7-12 move toward the higher brain wave of alpha with 8-12 cycles per second. They operate with a combination of absorbing information with their basic five senses and reflecting on their experiences from an increasing sense of self. They have the ability to interact with external data and be conscious of their separateness from their environments.

By age 12, most individuals show sustained periods of the higher brain wave activity beta, with 12-35 cycles per second, which indicates active, focused consciousness. This accounts for the increased capacity for adults and adolescents to concentrate and learn from external information.

Lipton writes, "By the time children reach adolescence, their subconscious minds are chock-full of information that range from the knowledge of how to walk, to the 'knowledge' they will never amount to anything, or the knowledge, fostered by loving parents, they can do anything they set out to do. The sum of our genetically programmed instincts and the beliefs we learned from our parents collectively form the subconscious mind…"

An understanding of brain wave activity casts a light on why young children are genuinely scared about monsters in their closets or under their beds. They are open to these suggestions because their young brains are moving in cycles close to hypnosis. Older kids come to understand that what they once believed as five-year-olds is not true. They cannot be convinced Santa Claus is real because their higher brain wave activity no longer matches the highly suggestive states of young childhood. Brain wave activity explains in part why kids think as they do. Changing brain wave activity underwrites the nature and capacity of what young people are able to learn at various stages.

THREE BRAINS

Cooper offers another way to consider the science of believing. Cooper joins the current scientific community in purporting that intelligence is not singularly centered in the brain as previous generations have believed; rather, it is distributed throughout the whole body. Human experience does not only process in our craniums he asserts, it also processes through the neurological networks of the intestinal tract and the heart.

Cooper writes that we have three brains—one in the head, one in the gut, and one in the heart. The intestinal tract contains approximately 100-million neurons (brain cells) and the heart brain, which acts independently from the head, is comprised of more than 40,000 nerve (or brain) cells. He states, "Every single heartbeat speaks an intelligent language to your whole body, a language that deeply influences how you perceive your world and how you react to it".

Cooper puts forward scientific evidence about these three brains. Even the simplest form of electrical firing creates a magnetic field around it, which can be measured. The magnetic field around the heart is five times greater than the magnetic field around the skull brain and gut brain. The heart's magnetic field extends approximately from fingertip to fingertip of an individual's outstretched arms, which tells us that the heart is a primary and powerful center of brain power.

Humans are constantly receiving information from their three operating brains. The cranium brain is not the only one that organizes and makes meaning from stimuli. The information gathered from body-based processing systems such as the heart and gut can be more accurate than information interpreted through the head brain. People report "gut feelings," or premonitions which turn out to be correct in spite of concrete or analytical data. When this happens, they are accessing information through their additional brains.

What children come to believe is a direct by-product of information processed by their hearts, minds and guts. Their identities are formed in their internal and external worlds, which include the information they have received from their environments, via these three powerful processing centers.

SHARED BRAINS

Part of what humans believe is within their individual bodies, and part is in the shared exchange with the body-brains of others. Siegel writes that the mind is distributed as a nervous system within the whole body and the mind regulates the flow of energy and information within the brain and between brains. This idea is evident in the common practice of a student asking another person for help. The student may ask, "What is 9x7?" When the other person starts to think about the question, the answer appears in the student's mind. What happened? The extra, shared brain power between them enabled the student to access the answer within themselves or it became available to the student through their shared energetic field. Quantum physics is giving us new understanding about the collective nature of the human brain, which impacts ourselves, others and the world at large.

CONDITIONED LEARNING

Kids are learning machines. They are learning about themselves in virtually every interaction in life. The process of "the outside becoming the inside" for young people occurs in part due to repetitive reinforcement. One very specific way children learn from their environments is through conditioned learning. There are two forms of conditioned learning: classical and operant. Young people's thinking is influenced by their reflexive adaptations to what happens around them—classical conditioning—and to the subtle or explicit system of reward and punishment in operant conditioning.

Classical conditioning was made famous through Pavlov's dog experiments in 1904. Pavlov noticed that dogs automatically salivated when presented with food, and also began to salivate when they saw white-coated lab assistants enter with food. Eventually, the dogs in his experiment began to salivate when lab assistants entered the room with or without food. Pavlov suggested that salivation in recognition of a white-coated lab assistant was a learned response called classical conditioning.

Classical conditioning is important for understanding what children believe because humans pair reflexive responses to their environments in the same way Pavlov's dogs salivated at the sight of research assistants. Stimuli combined with an internal, automatic response creates human classical conditioning and occurs regularly as people interact with their environments. For example, a loving parent repeatedly putting a child to bed, paired with the child calming in the process, trains the child's body to begin calming at bedtime, whether the parent is present or not.

Classical conditioning also occurs through trauma. Trauma trains the body to defend against certain stimuli, whether or not the body is in real danger. PTSD is classical conditioning because automatic, defensive reactions for safety occur in trauma when people experience being unsafe. Later, similar conditions or external cues, safe or not, remind the body to defend against trauma in the same way Pavlov's dogs salivated initially to food, but later salivated to lab assistants with or without food.

A common example of conditioned reflex in young people is the reaction they have when a parent returns from work. If the parent generally comes in with hugs and kisses delighting a youngster, the child will be positively conditioned to the parent's approach. Similarly, if a parent consistently interacts in a negative way, their arrival signals fear in the body of the waiting young person. Chemicals are released in these waiting youngsters in both scenarios. The learned association of a parent coming home, along with the positive or negative internal chemical reactions, continues to activate many years after their initial pairing and is a form of classical conditioning.

Classical conditioning is a very powerful teaching agent and is used to control behavior in positive and negative ways. It can be used to coerce and control others and it occurs automatically in sexual encounters when positive, reflexive chemicals are released in the body and come to be associated with individuals or circumstances. For example, the body's response to rape can send positive and negative reminders in subsequent sexual experiences.

Operant conditioning uses the same principle of pairing two simultaneous occurrences, but is based on deliberately training behavior in response to reward or punishment. It was named by Behaviorist B.F. Skinner in 1953. Skinner and fellow Behaviorists took a different approach to the study of human learning. Leaving out the idea of the mind or conscious thought, Skinner described human learning as simply a response to stimulus. In that system, certain responses could be solicited through reward or punishment.

For example, the toilet training method prescribed by Azrin and Fox, which aims to help children master toilet training in one day, is a generally successful, classic form of operant conditioning. To employ the method, an adult initially rewards the child when a doll successfully demonstrates wetting into a potty chair and moves toward rewarding the child with candy, praise, and delighted responses when the child urinates into a potty chair. This operant conditioning method occurs over several hours in a day and most often results in a child being well launched into the toilet training process by the end of the day.

Operant conditioning is a powerful agent for shaping beliefs, which takes place every day in homes where people live together. Ongoing overt or subtle responses to behavior send messages of approval and disapproval. The motivation to please a parent can be very constructive when toilet training, but parents can also use this motivation in a manipulative or destructive manner. For example, parents' goals for their children to overachieve academically or overperform in athletics can send a message to kids that they are not valuable unless they meet parental standards. Sometimes these expectations are appropriate to the young person's ability; other times they reflect a parent's over personalization of young people's performance. Kids are very aware of, and quite sensitive to, parental reaction. Even a caregiver's mood and other non-verbal signals are reward and punishment factors that train young people to behave according to the responses of others. Approval and disapproval are operant conditioning instruments that wield significant influence for youngsters.

NATURE OR NURTURE

Human development is shaped through nature and nurture. Children are born with unique temperaments and genetic predispositions and young people are greatly influenced by their environments. From the moment of birth, an infant is interacting with the environment by scanning for safety and eventually learning cultural cues for the best ways to get their needs met. The external environment trains the internal world of a young person, which combines with their natural style. Into the mix come the beliefs, behaviors and reactions of caregivers, all of which condition a young person's response.

As it relates to the science of believing, a young person's organic temperament influences their perspective in the learning lab of life. Biological makeup contributes to how kids perceive their worlds and what they come to believe as a result. When considering the idea, *you won't believe what your child is thinking*, caregivers have to consider a young person's natural disposition in order to understand how the child's behavior makes sense to them. A young person with a sensitive, caring temperament will interact in the world with a more compassionate view for others and may overly yield to others' needs. Such a youngster may hold a belief that others' needs are more important than their own. A competitive child by nature may come to believe that winning, or being better than others, is of great importance. Competitive behaviors will follow in order to maintain a positive sense of self. Competitive kids can turn play into competition, unaware that their perspectives about what is fun may not be in agreement with the beliefs of other young people. The temperament of an extroverted youngster will influence one way of acting and an introverted kid will be influenced in other ways. We have to accept that young people have different temperaments, and it is worthwhile to consider how those temperaments shape their beliefs.

SUMMARY

Many different sources influence a young person's developing belief system. Thinking is more than assent to certain ideas—it is the summation of nature, nurture, conditioned learning, environment, interpretation and the shared energetic field in which people live. Human cognition is a body-based, multi-layered phenomenon which begins before birth. Humans have brain cells in their heads, hearts and bellies, therefore their bodies are a source of learning and knowledge. What kids know comes primarily from their experiences, the interpretation they give to experiences and what they share with the bodies and brains of others. Some of this data is transferred directly from caregivers without words or intention, some is learned through conditioned learning, and most of it is interpreted through the naturally unique temperaments of kids. Throughout life, via this complex method of gathering and interpreting information, young people cannot help but transfer their 'outsides' into their 'insides', which become their beliefs and behaviors in the world.

Section One
Summary

As the title of this book suggests, caregivers may be surprised by the ways young people think about themselves and their circumstances. Once we understand how kids think, we can give them appropriate truth about themselves and their situations. Truth compassionately conveyed usually brings relief to young people who are using their interactions with the world as a feedback loop about themselves.

Every person possesses DNA that makes them a unique individual who relates to life through their own personality, family values and place on the globe. No matter where children live on the planet, they are influenced by their interactions with their environments. Through these interactions, young people develop understanding of themselves, others and the nature of life. Their understanding translates into beliefs—and especially beliefs about themselves—which may be right or wrong. Youngsters' ways of thinking can easily continue without re-evaluation into adulthood once they have been established.

Because no two youngsters are alike, there are limitless ways in which kids think. In these pages, I have offered four general concepts about how young people perceive themselves and relate to the world. Kids taught me these principles. Once I learned them, I checked with other young people who confirmed these ways of thinking were true for them as well. In review they are:

FOUR PRINCIPLES

1. Young people perceive the world with themselves at the center.

From this self-centered position, they use cause-and-effect thinking to understand their worlds, which can mean *I caused it.*

Toddlers through college-aged people are naturally the centers of their own worlds and can erroneously use cause-and-effect thinking to make sense of their experiences. Cause-and-effect thinking leads young people to believe that what happened to them was caused by them, even when they had no control over their circumstances or others' behavior. Kids can very easily misperceive they are at fault for life situations over which they had no influence simply because they were present or connected to a situation. They can wonder *why did this happen to me?* and derive incorrect answers because they view the world too simplistically. Until they develop broader perspectives, young people often blame themselves for the way life unfolds around them, suggesting *I caused it.*

2. Young people take words at face value.

They believe what they are told, which means *I believe it.*

Young brains have tremendous power and potential. The human mind does not present at birth as fully formed; it develops over time as young people mature. Initially, an infant's brain is operating at very low brain cycles, which increase as the human body develops. In the very young stages especially, but throughout the entire scope of development up to age 25, young people take at face value a majority of what they hear. Little kids believe cultural myths like Santa Claus and the tooth fairy, and all young people are expected to accept their educational curriculums into their mid-20's primarily at face value. Apart from academic instruction, young people also learn acceptable standards of behavior, ethics, racial biases, and the unlimited perspectives of others which come at them constantly during their developmental years. Young brains are at their peak for learning. Much of what kids learn will be ingested and absorbed directly from their environments. This tremendous intake process transfers a great deal of knowledge into the minds of young people and much of it is

130

taken at face value as presented. In a positive scenario, young people discover they are valuable, lovable and capable through this complex learning process. Many times, though, the information transferred and accepted by kids is negative and incorrect, which they do not have the experience or sophistication to discern.

3. Young people are prone to form "I am..." beliefs as a result of their experiences.

Converting an experience into one's identity means *I personalize it*. Many people are at risk for turning what they experience into information about themselves, but young people are especially at risk to form *I am* beliefs through their circumstances and interactions. Kids are always forming *I am* beliefs as they develop. Socio-economic status, popularity, grades, athleticism, physical traits, adults' behavior and many more conditions get translated into self-identity for young people. Virtually all negative and positive experiences have the potential to load into the conscious and unconscious minds of kids as something about themselves. These perceptions, true or not, influence how young people interact with the world, often for the remainder of life. Kids make choices based on what they believe they deserve, which is derived from interpretations about themselves, their families, and their environments.

4. Young people develop strategies in response to their situations.

Their strategies become life-long patterns, which means *I adapt to it*.

What to do about what happens? This dilemma is at the heart of how very young children through 20-somethings develop strategies to cope with life. In most cases, young people must have some response to the positive and negative circumstances around them. Youngsters adapt to life with their natural temperaments, levels of maturity, inherent abilities or other available resources. Some of their coping mechanisms are healthy and age-appropriate, while others are dysfunctional or self-harming. Addiction, self-cutting and social withdrawal may be negative strategies for responding to life, but positive qualities can be over used to a young person's detriment as well. Over-responsibility, over-helping, over-achieving, over-pleasing, or comfort seeking strategies

131

like over-eating and over-drinking are just a few of the many ways youngsters seek relief from their problems. Kids have three ways to deal with the challenges of life: healthy methods like seeking help, ignoring problems, or self-soothing to stabilize themselves in hard situations. Once developed, these behaviors can become ongoing patterns. The strategies we see operating in kids tell us about their stress, and their stress indicates it's time to understand their beliefs.

Collective Thinking

Truthful, healthy ways of thinking are evident in well-adjusted individuals. In order to help young people establish healthy ways of thinking, we have to understand how they are interpreting their interactions with culture, home environments, and the larger world because kids are prone to use their experiences as a feedback loop about themselves. Perception translates into beliefs—and especially beliefs about the self—which may be right or wrong. Youngsters' ways of thinking can easily continue without re-evaluation into adulthood once they have been established. A young person's collective thinking drives their behavior, life choices, and fulfillment in life.

Large and small traumas also influence children's thinking patterns. Minor traumas can often be effectively processed by helping kids understand and express the emotions of an experience. Other situations may require professional help.

Every day in the cauldron of life, young people are using the world's treatment of them to discover: *am I smart, stupid, lovable, likable, accepted, rejected, guilty, safe, worth keeping or a throw away?* Who knew kids were thinking like this? Adults may know that all children in the world are worthy of love and safe care, but young people may not know this invaluable truth until we discover what they are thinking and help them believe correctly.

Section Two which follows provides additional concepts and strategies for adults who interact with kids. The section includes ideas about shaping young people's behaviors, key components for successful parenting and more.

SECTION TWO

Perspectives

Chapter Seven

Fundamentals

Raising children is a complex task. When I first began parenting I thought no one could give me instructions on how to raise a child because no one else knew our precious son—he was a unique and special individual. Yet parenting guidelines seeped into the world we shared with other parents, including clear directions from new parent classes and literature from the hospital where our son was delivered. Five-and-a-half years later, after the birth of our third child at a different hospital, we were given a new set of directions for raising our newborn. Perspectives had shifted through a half decade and new viewpoints were dominant in the world of parental education. Our children grew, and the fashionable must-do-it-this-way guidelines from society continued to morph along with them. Each new class of parents felt strongly that their information was the essential information for raising healthy and successful offspring. Over those years, parental mandates shifted from never saying *no* to a child to sleep training infants. The mandates changed from very child-centered versions of parenting to greater parental control. Who was right?

More than three decades later, I write having parented infants, adolescents, and adult children, as well as counseling people of these same ages as a mental health professional. I have observed that some truths apply to most kids regardless of shifting parenting trends. Children have typical developmental stages and universal needs as they move from infancy to adulthood. From this platform, I present perspectives about what young people need in order for them to thrive in childhood and develop into fully functioning adults.

I believe it is important to keep in mind that each child is unique, and so are their caregivers. The alchemy between kids and those who raise them makes parenting more or less successful and satisfying to all parties. For example, introverted parents with highly extroverted children do not readily sync up regarding how many playdates are needed to keep their children happy. Apart from qualities like introversion or extraversion, there are ageless truths about what helps kids grow, develop meaningful relationships, and succeed educationally and vocationally.

My remarks here, borne out of experience, reflect viewpoints that align with contemporary parenting practices and some differ from shifting cultural ideas. For example, a current trend in parenting is to use time-out as a primary way to shape children's behavior. Although time-out is useful and appropriate in many contexts, I believe that drawing kids closer in many situations can be more effective than isolating them. This viewpoint is developed under the subheading *Time Out vs Time In*.

I also believe we are meant to transfer adult knowledge and skills to youngsters. In many ways, American culture lacks the framework for enabling one generation to transfer skills, experience and knowledge to the next generation, and I believe we are missing this tool as a positive way to influence young people. More will be said about these topics later.

It is clear young people of all ages need different things at different times. Some youngsters need direct emotional healing when they come to my office because they have been traumatized. With them, we use the tools of Lifespan Integration to heal their traumas and emotional issues. At other times, parents bring their children to counseling citing emotional problems, which could readily be solved by more effective parenting. These parents need support to better understand their kids and guidelines to make life better in the home and school. Some young people suffer because their parents make very self-centered and destructive choices, therefore kids need understanding and emotional support. Occasionally, families need help navigating painful family events or the special needs of family members. Kids and parents are unique. Their presenting issues are specific to them. Yet some common perspectives apply to young people of all ages, from most families, and my goal is to present viewpoints that will help young people get the support and encouragement they need to be successful in life.

FIVE FUNDAMENTALS

Five core concepts apply to toddlers through twenty-somethings, regardless of the decade, socio-economic status, or country of origin. The five principles are:

1. Children need food, shelter, safety and loving human connection. These are organic needs.
2. Children come into the world as unique individuals and attuned parenting considers their innate personalities.
3. Children need self-control.
4. In order to thrive, socially appropriate behavior is required in every stage of life.
5. Life takes effort. Success is achieved more through work than talent alone.

Adults are in the best position to equip young people with these components. Each of these fundamental principles will be discussed under its own heading. Additional suggestions for raising children follow these five core concepts.

FUNDAMENTAL ONE: CHILDREN NEED TO HAVE THEIR BASIC NEEDS MET

Plants wilt from lack of water and the solution to keeping a plant vibrant is regular care, including the right amount of water and nourishment. Children are also living beings whose only source of love and nourishment comes from adults who make sure their needs are met. All kids need food, shelter, safety and love-based human connection. Ideally, these basic needs are met by empathic caregivers who provide the ongoing essentials kids need in life.

Many sources speak to the importance of these basic human criteria. In 1943, Abraham Maslow presented a hierarchy which described the tiered nature of human needs. He presented a five-level pyramid that suggests physiological and safety needs are the most primitive, with higher needs coming into focus only when lower, more basic needs are met. According to Maslow, food, water, safety, and family are the essential requirements for human well-being. Unfortunately, these are unmet needs for some children in the 21st century, including in very developed cultures. We would be remiss to assume that all kids, even in well-resourced countries, have their basic needs met.

Young people become anxious and depressed when their primary needs are not fulfilled. School teachers face the challenge of educating kids who do not have their most basic needs met. A traditional saying proposes that one cannot philosophize on an empty stomach. Nor can one focus, learn, and be anxiety-free while living in dangerous and inadequate conditions. A third grade teacher commented that one of her most behaviorally challenged students was not functioning well in the classroom because he was not safe at home. Before she could teach him, she had to manage his behavior. In order to manage his behavior, she had to help him believe he was safe in her classroom.

The human race is designed to nurture and be nurtured within a social context. In addition to food, shelter, and safety, some children suffer from not having enough relational connection with the people around them. Humans are intrinsically social. Children are not meant to raise themselves—they need caregivers to meet their physical, emotional, and relational needs. Every human needs to be met on an emotional heart level and young people cannot thrive without this. A lack of human connection leads to hopelessness and despair, which is one of the markers for depression in children and adults.

Human connection is so vital it is essential for brain development. More than cells and hard-wiring compressed into a human skull, the brain is comprised of neuro-circuitry, which evolves within an intangible flow between people. Young brains are literally being shaped by exchanges with their caregivers. Experts report that mental and emotional regulation develops within the parent-child relationship, especially during the first four to six years of life. Kids develop trust and complex thinking generated from 'brain-sharing' with their caregivers. Ideally, this is a positive process in a setting where children's physical and emotional needs are met.

When young people do not have enough safety, nutrition, and human connection, they develop coping mechanisms. The coping methods learned at one stage in life can be repeated throughout the remainder of life. For example, underfed children may later horde food to defend themselves from scarcity even when their initial, difficult conditions have passed. If youngsters cannot trust that their emotional and physical well-being are important to caregivers, kids later neglect themselves or use the same negative behaviors with others. Young people determine their value from the attention and care they receive, which they often replicate in positive or negative ways for the rest of life.

Life's first fundamental is for survival—enough food, safety and human connection to go on living. When basic needs are met, people move on to the higher levels of Maslow's hierarchy, which include respect for others, creativity, morality and complex thinking.

FUNDAMENTAL TWO: CHILDREN NEED ATTUNEMENT AND RESPECT FOR THEIR UNIQUENESS

Most adults involved with toddlers through late adolescents agree that children come into the world with a natural bent. They are born with their own personalities, temperaments, preferences, and talents. Ideally, parents provide life's essentials for their offspring as mentioned above and do so with awareness to the unique personality of each child. Matching adult response to the temperament of individual kids is the learned process called attunement. Attunement is the ability to read and respond to young people's individual needs and parent them so their strengths become assets for a lifetime and their weaknesses are mitigated by learned appropriate behavior. Attunement reflects back to kids that they are valuable, their needs matter and their uniqueness is appreciated, at the same time requiring appropriate behavior from them. Attunement is not child-centered parenting in such a way adults become enslaved to their offspring or try to parent many children as if each were the only child in the family. Attuned parenting helps young people develop their innate qualities, not simply program kids into the objectives of their parents. To ignore a child's innate bent is to hamper their success in the world. A caregiver's function is to ask, "Who is this person and how can I help them be all they were created to be?"

Discovering children's personalities begins with reading infants' signals about their needs for sleep, food, holding or active time. Newborns through teenagers require varying amounts of social interaction and stimulation. Some kids are naturally interested in animals, science, or math, and others are energized by art or athletics. In addition, all young people need a certain degree of social connection, which naturally varies with the temperaments of individual children. Responding to the inherent tendencies and needs of kids throughout their growing up years will equip them with the skills to be self-attuned as they move into adulthood.

Parents discover that no two children are alike. Once caregivers achieve a certain degree of attunement to one youngster, they have to learn the temperament and individual needs of successive children. I propose that caregivers ask the question, *who is this child?* and move toward answering it through their decades of parenting. Knowing a young person is a fundamental component to raising them. No one will achieve perfect attunement to their offspring yet understanding youngsters' unique natures will enhance their health and success in life.

As mentioned, these fundamentals build upon one another. Attunement includes the previous truth that kids needs to have their basic needs met and the following fundamental that young people need to learn self-control within their families of origin.

FUNDAMENTAL THREE: CHILDREN MUST DEVELOP SELF-CONTROL

Self-control is essential for success in life. Self-control is the capacity to manage one's emotions and choose appropriate behaviors in a situation rather than act impulsively. Kids need to learn self-control and adults have the responsibility of teaching this important skill. Why is self-control important? Because no one wants to play with a child who cannot wait for a turn and throws tantrums when denied. Adults cannot fully enjoy or teach kids if they are tyrannized by a youngster who has not learned the essential life skill of self-management. Adults do not want to work with emotionally immature, self-centered co-workers. Virtually all people have the capacity to learn self-control and they need to do so if they are going to function well in society.

Self-restraint is learned at home. Parents have the responsibility to help youngsters develop the capacity to manage themselves when life does not go the way kids would like it to go. It can be hard for caregivers to weather the storms of resistance when children are not happy that their wishes are denied, but parents handicap kids if they fail to teach them the important skill of self-management in the face of disappointment. Adults may want to please kids in their care, or they may lack judgment regarding what kids needs, but caregivers and children alike suffer when pleasing young people preempts helping them achieve self-control. The short-term compromise of yielding to a young person's immature, self-centered behavior does not justify the long-term consequences for a young person who comes to believe the world is organized around their requests. Kids who come out of homes believing they are entitled to a certain level of service by others will be angry and lonely later in life.

Parents bring young people to my office for counseling citing emotional issues at school. It is not uncommon for a young child in this case to climb over the furniture in my office, demand things from the parent, repeatedly interrupt conversations, and be a major hindrance to productive interchange during the session. Adolescents have older versions of disrupting behaviors, such as being disrespectful and refusing to talk. Sometimes, but not always, the young person's presenting problem can be remedied by better emotional and behavioral self-control—skills that caregivers failed to require for various reasons. I am not sweeping all children into this category. I know people have true symptoms of ADHD and other diagnoses that present with similar characteristics. Yet I see kids who are suffering in social settings outside their homes because they have not learned to manage their emotions and behaviors. Their parents are suffering as well.

Some adults have been told to parent with a permissive model. As mentioned, our first baby came home from the hospital with literature explaining why parents should never say no to their children. Wanting to be a good parent and raise a good son, I dutifully followed the instructions that came with my child. Then he began to walk, talk, and exert his own wishes in unacceptable ways as two-year-olds do. Even though I was eager to get parenting right, the never-say-no strategy grated against intuitive parenting, and I began to think about the future for a child who could not tolerate hearing the unhappy word *no*. Against the teaching of the day, I found my inner compass and said no to never saying no. Our son was better for it. Some childish behaviors needed parental limits - not just options for being redirected—which was the suggested behavior management tool at the time.

Kids and adults suffer when the unreasonable demands of young people become too much. Adults begin to blame each other when life inside the family is not going well. Young people who have not developed self-control can become tyrants and strain the emotional and monetary resources inside families. Young people are disadvantaged with their peers and the world at large when their upbringing fails to teach them appropriate emotional and behavioral self-management.

Caregivers who yield to their children beyond reasonable limits do so because they cannot tolerate their children's disapproval or unhappiness. Cries of disappointment or tantrums bring parental adaptation instead of firmness with love. Yielding to young people's demands may seem easier in the moment, but not helping kids build emotional and behavioral self-control can strain relationships inside families for a long time. Adults grow resentful and disenchanted with uncooperative family members. Parents begin to avoid and withhold nurture due to the unpleasantness of their relationships with out-of-control children.

One way to help kids build self-control is to require that they manage themselves in difficult circumstances supplemented with parental soothing and support. A parent can say no and hold an unhappy youngster while they calm down from disappointment. Parents can respectfully feedback to a young child or teen what the young person wants as an indication the parent understands, and yet deny their wishes. Cries of "You don't understand!" are disempowered when an adult has communicated they do understand and the answer is still no.

Another way to help kids develop self-control and socially appropriate behavior is for adults to occasionally play games with them as a peer would play. This takes deliberate effort on the part of caregivers who hopefully don't care if they win at children's games or have the best action figure for play. It is good practice for kids to experience someone else winning at games and others getting what they want in social settings. If kids become upset when they are denied these things, parents can hold them with patience until they are able to re-engage the board game or play scenario. Even if it is later in the day after naps and mealtimes, requiring kids to re-engage with appropriate self-restraint teaches them one of life's most important skills—self-control. Kids without siblings especially need adult caregivers to interact with them this way. All young people need to learn cooperative, social behavior at home, which is built on managing one's self in the face of disappointment. Self-control builds resilience and resilience is a hallmark of well-being and success in life.

FUNDAMENTAL FOUR: AWARENESS OF OTHERS

Some young people are naturally sensitive to the feelings and wants of others. They come into the world with compassionate hearts and are mindful of others' feelings from the beginning of their lives. They are the preschoolers who offer their toys to others, the youngsters who comfort their classmates, and the teens who help other kids get what they want. Compassionate young people are moved by others' distress and want to do something to support them. When kids like these hear about large scale disasters, even very young children offer to send their money, clothing and blankets to needy people in faraway countries. Our planet is enriched by the caring, sensitive children and adults who naturally give their time, attention and resources to others. They do not have to be trained to be aware of others—they spontaneously gravitate to others' needs and attempt to meet them whenever possible.

Regarding the rest of the people on the planet, some young people need to be trained to understand the needs of others. Many kids need to be taught that others also want to have a turn and be successful at games. They need instruction that another person's experience in life is also important. Awareness of others does not happen automatically for many kids yet all young people need to develop the skill of understanding another person's world, at least in part. This life skill can be taught to preschoolers and teenagers alike. Parents are remiss if they neglect to equip kids with this essential life tool. Researchers have learned that the ability to relate to others is more important than intelligence for general success in life.

Self-control and the ability to relate well to others is an asset called *Emotional Intelligence* (EQ). Adults and kids alike can be taught EQ, which is an art and a skill. EQ is the art of awareness and understanding what others might want, need and feel. EQ requires the skill of self-management, which includes regulating one's emotions and reactions, instead of a quick, self-centered emotional response. Emotional intelligence is not the complete acquiescing of self. Instead, it is the capacity to choose behaviors and responses which take into account others and one's self. EQ involves the capacity for empathy, which is generally defined as compassion and understanding of another person.

Adults can help children develop emotional intelligence by training them in the skill of empathy. This practice involves direct conversations about other kids' needs and wishes, joined with guidance toward behaviors that reflect awareness of others. Parents with only one child must help them develop this capacity, since an only child does not have the family learning lab of other siblings whose needs and preferences also matter. EQ can be learned and kids will suffer without it.

Selfish people suffer due to their inability to socially engage the experiences of others. Young people may grow up naturally self-centered because no one has taught them the skill of being other-oriented at times. The narcissists of the world are often confused by their lack of social intimacy. They may have accomplishments, financial success, and impressive careers, but they are often lonely and ashamed. Wealth and success cannot buy them true community, which is built on healthy intimacy. Self-centered people miss the nurture of interpersonal relationships because they have not learned how to assess and meet the needs of others.

144

Unfortunately, they do not understand the give and take of successful interpersonal exchange.

For example, a 23-year-old man organized a trip with friends and controlled everything about their travel. In our counseling session, he expressed confusion and anger that his friends seemed to be unhappy with him on the trip. "Everything I did just made the most sense," he explained. Unfortunately, he was unable to organize an event which included the ideas and preferences of others.

Selfish and controlling people suffer loneliness because others avoid them. When kids lack basic training in emotional intelligence, they suffer later in life because it is hard to be happy without positive relationships. The skills for positive, healthy relationships can be learned any time in life.

Young people, like the client mentioned above, have very often been the recipients of caregivers who did not take seriously their children's thoughts, emotions and wants. Attunement to young people teaches them that their emotions and internal worlds are important, which is not the same as spoiling kids. Young people who have received attunement learn to track and manage their own thoughts and feelings, which is a natural bridge to understanding other people's thoughts, feelings and desires.

Awareness of others is the basic capacity to perceive what it might be like to be the other person in a situation. For preschoolers, this means knowing that other children also want to be first in line or have a turn on the swings. For middle schoolers, emotional intelligence reflects an understanding that others want to be included and liked. For high school students, EQ means showing positive regard toward others as well as positive regard toward one's self. Paying attention to others works well in every stage in life.

If kids do not have natural tendencies to consider the feelings and wants of others, caregivers will be the primary resources for helping young people develop these abilities. To some youngsters, it may come as a surprise that other kids want what they want. When young people of all ages struggle to have successful friendships and social opportunities, it is generally because they have not developed the skills to consider a situation from the perspectives of others. Parents can teach the social skill of knowing what others might be thinking or feeling in situations. Resources are available for learning this essential life skill.

FUNDAMENTAL FIVE: SUCCESS TAKES EFFORT

Young people need the capacity for sustained effort. The ability to maintain a course of action is required for success, and this trait is a greater predictor of achievement than intelligence. Adults at home and school train kids to develop this ability. Educators find youngsters with an open mindset and a willingness to work can accomplish more than their counterparts who have a fixed idea about their intelligence and capabilities. For example, kids who don't believe they are smart often give up and fail to put forth the effort to be successful. On the other hand, young people considered smart may coast through school without putting forth much effort, and collapse when hard work is required. It is not uncommon for smart, successful students to fail out of college when they have to try harder for academic achievement than they did in their earlier schooling. Carol Dweck, author of the culture-changing book *Mindset,* asserts, "...human qualities, such as intellectual skills, could be cultivated through effort."

Life takes effort and success often takes extended effort. Talent is not a substitute for the work it takes to accomplish goals and complete the tasks of life. Michelangelo, the 15th century Italian artist, is an example of a man who used his talents, plus sustained effort, to accomplish meaningful outcomes—including outcomes in areas that were not his preferences. Michelangelo painted the Sistine Chapel from 1508 to 1512, a project he did not enjoy.

Michelangelo considered himself a sculptor, not a painter. Additionally, he worked in uncomfortable positions, standing beneath the ceiling while painting over his head for four years. The Sistine Chapel, and Michelangelo's other great works, are a result of his talent—and sustained effort—in spite of challenges and personal preferences.

Different forms of praise affect children's willingness to put effort into their work. Praise and encouragement for kids to bounce back from failure and work harder teaches them persistence. Praise for doing any aspect of an assigned task reinforces young people's progress in the right direction. The brain rewards people for continuing to work for an outcome with its feel-good chemical dopamine. Intermittent reward is required in order to reinforce dopamine release. Dr. Robert Cloninger at Washington University in St. Louis states, "A person who grows up getting too frequent rewards will not have persistence, because they'll quit when the rewards disappear." The brain has to learn that frustrating spells can be worked through, and rewards will be realized later.

Not all praise motivates kids to put forth effort. Praise such as, "You're smart, you're talented, everything comes easy to you," is ineffective praise. It does not reward the work required to accomplish things in life. Dweck and others found that young people frequently praised for their innate talents, rather than their effort, are competitive, seek image maintenance, and are unwilling to support their peer's accomplishments.

American culture is emerging from a trend which has been heavy on praising kids for their talents and performance. Instead, young people need to be coached to develop the ability of sustained effort and trying again. Seldom are meaningful and sustainable outcomes achieved quickly. Even the smartest individuals must develop the discipline of hard work and the capacity to rebound in the face of failure. Most kids can succeed when trained to keep working and trying again when disappointed. Instead of relying on talents alone, young people need to develop internal strength for exerting effort in order to reach their potentials.

Those who learn to keep working become better group members than those who do not learn this skill. Children and adults find themselves in group settings in virtually every context—school, work, social settings, or at home. Cooperative group members understand that effort is required to maintain group functions and to meet the group's goals. Young people who work effectively toward group goals will be rewarded in life with appreciation and advancement. Supervisors often choose a hard worker over a more talented one. Employers are looking for individuals who can work hard, cooperate with co-workers, and be self-directed. These qualities are developed initially in childhood by adults who teach kids that sustained effort is required of them. Learning to apply one's self—whether it is pleasant or not—increases the chance of success in academic, social and work settings. Sustained effort is not always directly rewarded, but it is a developed character trait which will provide significant returns throughout life.

Achieving the Five Fundamentals

A resource I recommend for helping young people achieve the fundamentals outlined above is the parenting book *Calmer, Easier, Happier Parenting: Five Strategies That End the Daily Battles and Get Kids to Listen the First Time* by Noel Janis-Norton. The author has had the opportunity to ask caregivers around the globe what they want for their children. Regardless of culture or location, parents essentially named the same fundamentals I have discussed in this text: basic needs met, individuality, self-control, awareness of others and the capacity for sustained effort. Janis-Norton uses different phrases to name these basic elements, but the concepts appear to be universal. Janis-Norton's list, compiled from world-wide audiences, includes cooperation, confidence, motivation, self-reliance and consideration. Janis-Norton writes, "These are the traits that will help children enjoy their families, make and keep friends, reach their potential at school, and eventually find satisfaction as adults in the areas of relationships, careers and leisure pursuits."

Janis-Norton leads parents through a step-by-step guide for helping young people develop these basic characteristics. Her method is based on teaching young people what they need to do and reinforcing the teaching with manageable and respect-ful techniques. The title of the book speaks to the goals of par-enting: creating environments where youngsters are cooperative and learn the fundamental skills for successful living in a setting where struggle is minimized and adults can enjoy the young peo-ple in their care.

BLUE RIBBON PARENTING

In a very well-known and often-cited project, psychologist Di-ana Baumrind conducted a study on more than 100 preschool-age

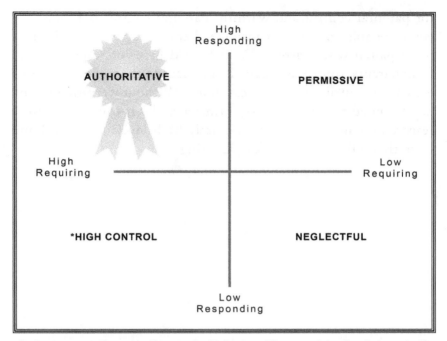

Authoritarian is Baumrind's term for high control/low requiring but it is so similar to Authoritative, the author has chosen to represent the quadrant as High Control.

children. Her work is still considered the gold standard for effective parenting today. Baumrind's research evaluated two axes of parenting, which she named *Demandingness* and *Responsiveness*. *Demandingness* evaluated the degree of control adults exerted and the level of behavior they required from their children. It is reflected in the following graph with the updated term *Requiring*—a synonym I have chosen for Baumrind's *Demandingness*.

The *Responsiveness* category described the extent to which parents supported individuality, self-assertion and cooperated with young people's needs and requests. *Responsiveness* evaluated adult warmth, sensitivity and attunement. It is indicated on the graph as *Responding*.

The Parenting Sweet Spot

Baumrind's study indicates that the most effective parenting style exhibits high requiring and high responding, which she termed Authoritative parenting. It was the highest scoring quadrant for parental control and warmth. Parental control is needed for young people to learn to manage themselves yet control needs to be paired with warmth. With high degrees of responsiveness from parents, youngsters learn attunement to themselves and others which contributes to success in life. Without warmth, kids are handicapped to develop trust, intimacy and self-love. Baumrind's research quantifies that appropriately high levels of control and warmth are the sweet spot of parenting.

Chapter Eight
Recommendations

The first section of this book speaks to the idea *you won't believe what your child is thinking* and suggests ways for adults to respond to this dilemma. In addition, other ways young people think have been discussed and five fundamentals for what kids need have been presented. This chapter includes additional ideas to support caregivers and further help young people and their families thrive. The themes overlap with the five fundamentals from the previous chapter, but the ideas presented below bear viewing from another lens because they are critical to young people's success and development.

FILLING UP WITH LOVE

Kids need love! They thrive where love is present and they languish where it is absent. Young people who are well loved have internal reserves to withstand life's many challenges. No youngster will be loved perfectly, but those who are raised where love is present learn it is safe to venture into the world to share their gifts, talents and intelligence with others.

Beyond experiencing love from others, love is as available as air and I have had the opportunity to teach children how to fill their hearts with love from a universal source. It only takes a few quiet moments to access this ever-available resource and fill their hearts to capacity. No one has to be deprived of this essential fuel for living. To fill their hearts, I ask kids to close their eyes and imagine where love comes from. I tell them love is ever-present and all they have to do is fill up with it like a car fills up with gasoline. Love is not dependent on people or their behavior. Love is always ready to come pouring into their hearts when they open up to receive it.

Generally, I ask youngsters to share how they imagine love is going to come into their hearts. A 13-year-old boy said he imagined a small fire in his heart, like a campfire. As he focused on receiving love, the fire grew bigger and his heart grew warmer. After a couple of minutes his chest was so warm he had to throw off his jacket. Later he told me that every time he filled up with love his heart became warm and he felt more peaceful and less afraid. A ten-year-old boy said he imagined he reached for something like the pump at a gas station and filled his heart until it was full. He practiced this image at bedtime or on the bus to school. He always had better days when he started the school day with his heart full of love. No matter which visual they use, young people can always tell me when their hearts are partially full, almost full or completely full of love. Many people physically feel warmth in their hearts when doing this exercise.

I encourage kids to fill up with love every day using the image that works best for them. When youngsters' hearts are full of love they are calmer, more cooperative and better at relating to others. A lack of love creates low self-esteem and drives many of the behaviors we find challenging in young people. Low self-esteem can cause people to be negative, discouraged, non-cooperative and overly seeking of attention. Deprivation affects human thinking. When extra love is added to young people's lives, things turn out better for them. They become less reactive and able to see the needs of those around them—not just their own needs. Teaching kids to get a full serving of love every day from a resource that is always available wherever they are, helps youngsters function better in the world. Even though caregivers may love their children very much, generally, a few adults and peers cannot fully satisfy the human need for love.

I suggest kids fill up with love at bedtime, in the morning, or any time things aren't going well for them. It only takes a few moments to fill a heart so there is no reason for children to be lacking love when it is available to them from an endless source. Unfortunately, most people do not know about the endless supply of love we can draw into our hearts at any time, so I think it is important to share with others, especially children, this wonderful resource that will improve their lives.

VALIDATION REVISITED

Validation, a concept discussed in chapter four, also fits into the blue ribbon quadrant of Authoritative parenting (high requiring and high responding). One way to shape young people's behavior is to validate kids for their thoughts and emotions, while requiring appropriate compliance from them. Validation is the interpersonal skill of stepping out of one's perspective for a moment, finding some wisdom and understanding in a another's viewpoint, and reflecting back that understanding.

Validation expresses compassion for a youngster's wants at the same time an adult requires something other than what the child is seeking. Parents can demonstrate understanding and compassion toward young people who are angry, sad or in despair at thwarted desires. Validating the feelings and perspectives of kids, even when their perspectives differ greatly from those of an adult, helps stabilize them. This form of communication conveys respect and understanding for another person's inner world and helps them sort out feelings and drives. We all long to be understood, and validation mirrors the inner world. When kids feel validated, they can usually release their intense wish to get what they want, or they can hear the word "no" and still feel valued. Validation sends the message *even when you can't have your way you matter as a person because you are heard and understood.*

Validation is acceptance and nonjudgmental feedback about the other person's reality. Expressed with empathy, validation can be a form of high warmth from Baumrind's most successful parenting quadrant. As part of this parenting style, caregivers can validate young people's thoughts and feelings yet also be kind, firm, and clear about requirements for their behavior. Examples of this type of validation are:

1. "Being with your friends seems like the most important thing in the world. Teenagers want to be with their friends most of the time and it proba-

bly seems unfair that we won't let you stay over-
night at Melissa's when her parents aren't home.
When Melissa's parents are home you can have a
sleepover, but not tonight."

2. "I know you want the new bike. It's really awesome and I like it, too. We did not come into the
store to buy a bike and we are going to leave in just
a minute. You need to have a good attitude when
it's time to leave."

In summary, the purpose of validation is to name as accurately as possible the thoughts and feelings of another person.
Following a young person's lead into their inner world provides
emotional dialysis to help them understand thoughts, feelings and
desires. Even if a sincere, but incorrect guess is offered, the recipi-
ent of validation will usually make a correction and state their experience more clearly. One of the most powerful gifts parents can
give their children is the reflection of being known. Validation
recognizes that children have thoughts and feelings which matter.

Validation is not agreement; nor is it flattery and manipula-
tion. As it applies to young people, validation means grownups
understand what's going on for them and also make the best,
empowered adult decisions for their benefit.

Hall and Cook wrote a guidebook to parental validation
I recommend titled *The Power of Validation: Arming Your Child
Against Bullying, Peer Pressure, Addiction, Self-Harm and Out-of-
Control Emotion.* The book provides instructions for the reader
and a strong argument for the role of validation for children. John
Gottman (as cited in Hall and Cook) states, "In general, validated
children perform better in school, get along better with friends
and others, contract fewer infectious illnesses, are more resilient
in parent conflict, and grow to become more self-confident adults.
They also seem better to able to comfort themselves. In fact, validation seems to improve overall development."

Validation is a gift to virtually everyone. When I say to adults
and kids, "It feels bad because it is bad" they often reply, "Do
you really think so?" They are looking for validation that it is
okay to be upset about something upsetting. Unfair, unkind, and

154

unfortunate circumstances happen to everyone. Concurring that something is not right and feels badly gives people permission to admit what they already think and feel. When children hear "It feels bad because it is bad," they usually respond with relief and expand on what is troubling them. Affirming that it is normal to be upset about something difficult can be the entry point to solving problems. Acknowledging something is hard does not give license to endless self-pity. Instead it offers kids and adults reassurance when we kindly affirm, "It feels bad because it is bad."

FORMULA FOR SOCIAL SUCCESS

No parent wants to hear the painful cry, "Nobody likes me. No one wants to play with me." These gut-turning statements often reflect a degree of shame and hearken back to a parent's own success or failure with social relationships, which can make it hard for adults to be objective and helpful responding to a youngster's cry.

Social connection in life matters and it is important to help young people understand how to be socially engaged. Depending on an adult's experience, caregivers can be overly dismissive to the young person's complaint or overly involved trying to solve the problem. Appealing to a teacher will not solve a social problem if kids cannot use the fundamental behaviors for getting along with others.

According to Marano, a simple three-part formula applies to all social success. The rubric for positive relationships is the same across age, circumstances, and financial strata. The natural temperaments of extraversion and introversion do not override the general components that make for positive relationships. The three-part formula for social success as defined by Marano is:

1. The ability to self-regulate emotions.
2. Awareness of the needs and experiences of others.
3. The capacity to generate positive interactions, which take into account self and the other.

Many youngsters naturally fall into success with all three elements, but often kids need to be taught these key components. This rubric for social success applies regardless of age. If a young child or older adolescent is struggling in social settings, one or all of these three qualities needs to be further developed. The guidelines can be taught to kids and practice helps them increase their ability for using them.

1. The Ability to Self-Regulate Emotions

The first social success component is the capacity to manage one's emotions. Studies indicate a strong parallel between a young person's ability to regulate emotions and popularity. Emotional regulation is appropriately managing a broad spectrum of feelings while tolerating delayed gratification. If kids cannot emotionally self-regulate, they can become overwhelmed, aggressive or withdraw from social contact. Emotional arousal hampers the capacity for processing information accurately and maintaining awareness of others. Self-regulation is a learned behavior strongly guided by adults.

Emotional regulation develops initially as parents soothe their infants and young children. To do this, caregivers recognize and in some cases name feelings, express compassion and validate what is going on for kids. Ideally, adults would help to emotionally regulate youngsters without shaming them. Over time, young people transfer the external experience of being soothed to an inward mechanism of self-soothing. They develop self-management muscles to do for themselves what caregivers have extended to them, thus learning the skill of emotional regulation.

Social success requires the ability to make positive responses in the face of disappointments, which can only occur if young people can manage their emotions. Caregivers are strong models of social behavior. Kids often develop emotional regulation and social behaviors similar to the adults in their lives. Helping young people learn delayed gratification and self-regulation means adults need to give them opportunities to wait for a turn, extend help to others and face disappointments with appropriate behavior. These opportunities help kids develop the skills of self-regulation as a precursor to understanding the needs of others.

In addition to parental soothing and modeling, another way to help youngsters develop self-regulation is through coaching in live situations. When conflicts arise, adults can coach young people with the exact words to say in order to help them gain

156

self-management in the moment. Direct coaching gives young-sters options beyond withdrawal, tantrums or aggressive behavior. It might seem odd to adults, but young people are quite able to repeat verbatim what an adult tells them to say to another person. Kids of all ages are relieved when they receive help and accomplish the three-step process of social success, which they cannot always generate on their own.

Social coaching is not limited to young children, although the following example comes from a preschool classroom. I worked with Jeremy who was many months younger than most of the children in his pre-kindergarten classroom. Jeremy was still struggling with the basic rules of good behavior several months into the school year. He interrupted other children's activities and threw their projects onto the floor when they would not let him join them. The students and teachers were frustrated by his behavior.

I helped Jeremy by following him around the preschool classroom and whispering the appropriate words to say or actions to take in various situations. He copied my words exactly.

When Jeremy approached a table where two girls were cutting paper, he grabbed their scissors and attempted to leave. The girls were upset and expressed their frustration that Jeremy could not be trusted when he was nearby. I put my hand on Jeremy's hand and guided him to replace the scissors on the table. I said, "The girls are using these scissors. You need to say, 'Can I borrow these scissors?'"

With my hand on his and the scissors firmly planted on the table, Jeremy said, "Can I borrow these scissors?"

The girls turned toward him and pleasantly said, "Okay." They were happy to share their scissors and their angst at his aggression quickly turned into cooperation when Jeremy did what was socially appropriate.

Like these girls, the other children in the classroom never balked at my presence when I whispered exactly what Jeremy should say or do. Other children responded directly to him and seemed relieved that they could finally play with Jeremy the way they played with other kids. Although the teachers had been quite concerned that Jeremy did not have the self-restraint and emotional maturity to move onto the next level of education, as a result of the teachers' sustained effort and my direct coaching, Jeremy's social competency increased and the teachers recommended him for kindergarten.

Preschoolers through adolescents benefit from direct coaching. Some parenting experts advocate for kids to learn from their mistakes, which is a parenting style with a place in the repertoire of choices. Yet in many cases like Jeremy's, no amount of learning from mistakes would have produced the results direct coaching delivered. Jeremy was too immature to learn directly from his ineffective behavior. After several months of tyrannizing the classroom, Jeremy had not developed appropriate social behavior even though the teachers had instructed all the children in what was expected of them. Jeremy needed remedial training in the rules and behaviors of acceptable social interaction.

Self-regulation is the foundational piece upon which social success is built. Caregivers need to be mindful that young people's capacity to self-regulate is one of the most important skills they can develop in life, so it is worth the time and the effort required for young people to understand and apply this essential life skill.

2. Awareness of the Needs and Experiences of Others

The second component of social success takes into account what might be happening for others. Regardless of age, people need to recognize social and emotional cues, which lead to understanding the emotional states of others. Empathy is the ability to discern what another person is feeling by interpreting their words, facial expressions and body language.

Pro social behavior includes responding to another's distress, offering social invitations, providing an explanation when turning down a request, and other similar gestures that suggest positivity toward another. Humans are innately designed to live in social groups. The need for safe inclusion in social groups is biological and universal. Therefore, behaviors that suggest inclusion to others meet an intrinsic, social need. Also, individuals who excel at empathy and communicating value to others excel in the areas of social success. Kids who are strong in prosocial behavior are well-liked and usually quite successful. Developing capacity for positive social behavior, which is built on awareness of others, correlates to success in life.

3. Generating Alternatives that Consider Self and the Other

The third component of social success follows after young people have learned to emotionally self-regulate and discern what is happening for others. It is the skill of generating ideas pertaining to the needs and wishes of both parties. Some youngsters will automatically yield when differences of opinion rise between themselves and their friends. Other young people will dominate and control the direction of play to get what they want. Relationship fluency is not accomplished by demanding, over-yielding, or controlling a situation. The socially successful young person offers ideas and keeps working with a situation until a mutually satisfying outcome has been reached.

A socially competent person will find ways to include the ideas and preferences of others, while holding onto their own values and needs. They can generate ideas and solutions by contextually understanding the other person and brainstorming potentially satisfying results. Successful adults do this to a more complex degree than young people, but the method is the same. In order to have satisfying, ongoing relationships, individuals must learn to consider the needs and wants of others along with their own wishes, think creatively about mutually satisfactory ideas, while maintaining emotional regulation.

This formula for social success is so simple a four-year-old can do it, which some do naturally. Other children need to be taught the steps for social success. When young people understand the basic formula, they can use the recipe throughout their lives. Examples of the three-step process of social success are:

- **The preschooler who notices a classmate standing nearby and watching while children color at a table.** A socially successful preschooler asks, "Would you like to color with us? You could sit here and use these crayons." This example portrays the willingness to yield the exclusivity of the coloring group

159

(self-regulation), an awareness that a child watching might want to participate (empathy), and the invitation for the child to join the table (a generative, collaborative idea).

- **Kids on the elementary school playground who argue about whether to play soccer or football at recess.** Socially successful kids recognize that soccer and football are both important (self-regulation even if they have a strong preference). A student with emotional intelligence may suggest playing football one day and soccer the next day; or football at morning recess, and soccer after lunch (generative suggestion). Some kids in the group may want to play only soccer or only football. The socially successful youngster will collaborate and play soccer some days and football on other days, even if they have preferences for one sport over the other (empathy for the experience of others).

- **Teenagers trying to decide what to do for fun or which movie to watch.** Adolescents can spend a good amount of time thinking and talking about what to do next. Socially successful teens use the same process mentioned above. They hold an openness to watch a movie, which might not be their first choice (self-regulation), make suggestions about movies (generating ideas), and participate when the idea of watching a movie gets replaced by a different activity that may not be the teen's first choice (considering the self and others).

A fine point is evidenced in these examples. Walking away and refusing to participate is not an ingredient of social success in most cases. Generally young people who refuse to play unless their demands are met are not socially successful. Remaining in a group and being a cooperative group member—even when a young person's ideas are not accepted—is an important skill for building social currency. Seldom can kids achieve social belonging without participating in support of others. How kids decline to participate is also important to their social success. Reflecting empathy toward others and giving a reason for declining are two keys to saying no.

Young people need social competency in order to be successful. These are natural traits for some kids, but many youngsters, including teens, need to be taught the skills of social and emotional intelligence. When young people are struggling with friendship issues or adults are not enjoying the company of the youngsters in their care, usually at least one of the above components is being under-used. Caregivers can help kids be socially adept by teaching them the above steps and helping them practice.

In summary, social competency is a three-pronged skill arising from the ability to self-regulate emotion, understand the inner states of others, and bring creativity to a situation to make it satisfying for all the participants. Without social aptitude, kids will be confused about why others do not want to engage with them. Everyone needs the tools to enjoy and be connected to a network of human relationships throughout their lives.

ADOLESCENTS
Toddlers in Big Bodies

Teenagers are going through the same developmental tasks as two-year-olds. Teens need from their parents the same support, encouragement and limits toddlers require. One way to respectfully think of teens is like toddlers in big bodies. This idea is a supportive description and not in any way a negative connotation about teenagers whom I respect as enjoyable and interesting people.

If parents recollect life with a toddler, they will remember that two-year-olds exert more personal autonomy as more of who they are internally unfolds. Personality emerges to a greater degree in toddlerhood, and two-year-olds send the message to caregivers, *love me, support me, don't disagree with me, and let me be who I am. I'm going to be unhappy with you if you thwart me in any of these areas.* In many ways, these are also the attitudes and behaviors of adolescents. Because adolescents are moving for a second time through the developmental stages mentioned here, teens need the same responses from their parents that toddlers need—validation, support for their separateness, boundaries in the face of immaturity, love, respect and confidence that teens will keep maturing, while enjoying them for who they are in the present. For this reason, I respectfully suggest that caregivers can get somewhere near 'right' in the parenting of teenagers if they will provide the same love and limits that were needed when their kids were toddlers.

Launching—Getting Out of Parental Gravity

Adolescents send the message they are trying to get out of a parent's gravity. If we consider the family as a group who lives on its own planet—with its own gravitational force—we would understand that the developmental task for teenagers is to get out of the gravitational pull which has kept them connected and safe on the planet where they grew up. Ideally, a child arrives into a family group and the adults make sure the child is rooted and their needs are met. As kids move into adolescence, they begin to contemplate where they want to live, what they might want to do for work, how they will parent when they have children, and other ways they will do things more progressively and effectively than their caregivers. Most teenagers become emotionally and physically healthy enough to move into this developmental stage because an internal force within them is rising and thrusting them toward adulthood. The movement to get out of a parent's gravitational pull is an internal, natural drive toward independence.

At the same time, knowing that humans need connection, the problem of trying to provide this support to adolescents during their launch phase is that teens rebuff caregivers one moment and need them a moment later. It is tempting for parents to feel hurt by the mixed messages adolescents send. Being humans themselves, parents may think, *Fine! You separate from me and I will separate from you.*

Even though individuation and separation is the developmental task of adolescence, generally, parents should not turn off the gravity machine and send their young flying untethered into adulthood. Teens benefit by the growth, practice, and evolution, which occurs as they mature into adulthood within the structured support of caregiving adults. I am advocating here for parents not to reactively create emotional distance from their adolescents because they are hurt by a teenager's emotional separation from them. Teens appear to not need the protection of adults in their lives. Yet instability from their rapid, internal changes means adolescents very much need the mature, emotional framework caregivers can provide. Teens need a foundational stability at all times; not just at the times they appear to need it.

Validate the Adolescent

Validation has been discussed in previous contexts, but it has a unique meaning in the parallel between teens and toddlers. When a two-year-old approaches an adult with a toy in hand, the toy is extended toward the adult with a phrase such as, "Truck." The response evoked from the adult who receives the toy is a validating, "Truck," at which point the toddler indicates the toy should be returned and the exchange is complete. Moments later, the toddler may return with another item, hand it to the adult, name it, wait for a validating response, and take back the item. This is a universal, developmental phase, which generates validation for two-year-olds. Handing the item to the adult has nothing to do with the child's wish for the adult to keep it. Instead, the exchange reinforces the child's perspective. With toddlers, we generally participate in the exchange with ease and do not take personally their need to maintain control of the object and evoke validation from us.

Teenagers are in the same accelerated growth phase with the same self-discovery process occurring for them. They, too, long to evoke validation from others around them. They suggest a perspective—an idea for how the world looks from their viewpoints - and they want to be taken seriously for what they have discovered. They are not offering their discovery for others to keep; they are sharing it so their discovery will be reflected back to them as they continue exploring their worlds.

The immature, self-centered validation stage of two-year-olds does not last if adults engage in the natural process. Toddlers outgrow it when caregivers respond appropriately and keep a two-year-old's maturation processes evolving. Similarly, teenagers need to be heard and taken seriously for what they think. This response does not mean adults have to agree with adolescents—it means teenagers who receive responses of respect and care are being given the right conditions to evolve and develop their own ideas and perspectives. Knowing one's self is a critical component to successfully being in the world. For a teenager, knowledge of self is the beginning of functioning in the world as an independent individual moving toward adulthood.

I suggest adults who share lives with adolescents validate them when it is possible. Just like toddlers who extend a toy and say, "Truck," teenagers offer their new ways of thinking and want respectful responses in return. Rather than argue or dismiss a teen's perspective when it is shared, adults can engage the viewpoints of adolescents and ask why they think as they do, how they see their perspectives affecting the broader world and other conversations that cause the teenager to deepen their thinking. The need for reinforcement of new, young perspectives is a developmental phase for teenagers, just as it is for toddlers. Meeting this phase with respect and care helps young people continue growing toward adulthood.

Staying the Course

Quitting too early is one of the ways adults do a great disservice to their teenagers. I observe that some caregivers are inclined to give up parenting when adolescents exert a great deal of their individual selves, which is their primary pathway to adulthood as mentioned. In such a case, parents may throw up their hands and no longer provide connection and boundaries yet teens need adults to continue setting limits and engaging with them throughout their last laps of childhood. Until adolescents consistently demonstrate an adult level of responsibility and self-control, caregivers need to stay involved helping teens internalize the truth that the world requires limits to their behavior. Parents are very important people in the lives of teenagers. Pleasing a parent who is invested in a child is actually a strong motivator for all young people, including adolescents, who might not communicate the importance of their relationship to a parent. Parental disapproval is one of the most powerful deterrents to teenagers considering poor choices. Parents don't usually give up on toddlers, nor should they remove themselves from teens just because teenagers seem like they are not interested in influence from adults.

Women sometimes feel they no longer have influence as parents when sons get taller and stronger than their mothers. It is a misperception to assume that mothers are no longer impactful as parents. When I encounter moms who feel this way, I share a phrase I used when one of my boys was over six feet tall and still growing at 15 years old. I knew my words would only be required until his emotional maturity caught up with his physical development. I occasionally mentioned to him that "I was still taller on the inside than he was on the outside." It was a clear, but loving reminder that I was still in the role of parenting and I had not given up caring about the choices he made. Size did not equal adulthood and I intended to stay on the job of helping him internalize important values and choices.

Men and women need to parent their teenage children, and each of them can do it alone if necessary. Kids need to be parented all the way through adolescence. Important adults create a widening frame for teenagers to develop and explore. Opening the gate and letting teens run free can give them too much untethered opportunity if teen maturity does not match good judgment. Parents are the boundary setters and gate managers, enjoying teens as they develop and mature. Just like toddlers, adolescents continue to need the presence of adults who will validate them, appreciate them, and let them develop into their truest selves, within the framework of safe, expanding environments.

Remain Close

I observe that adolescence is a time when parents may not understand the importance of their presence and relationship to teenagers. Simply having a parent in the building is a reassurance to young people, even if they do not converse or politely interact with the adult throughout an entire evening. Ideally, caregivers represent safety to teens even though there are times when teenagers would prefer to have the run of their parent's home without adults present. Two parents told me they made a commitment to be home on Friday and Saturday nights as often as they could when their children were going through the teen years. It somewhat hampered their own independence, but they felt it created a safety net for their teenage kids and a place where friends could be together under quasi-supervision. These parents appreciated newfound freedom when their sons and daughters went away to college or began to live on their own.

Another method to provide relational closeness to a fairly unresponsive teen is to sit in the same room where the teen is watching television, reading a book, or working on a project. Even if very little dialogue takes place between caregiver and child, the message is sent that the youngster is not alone. I have heard from parents that when they follow this suggestion, a silent, sulking teenager will often begin a conversation about the television program or something else interesting to them. A wise parent will use this opportunity to engage a teenager with conversations that lead the young person to further reveal what they are thinking rather than for a parent to be authoritative about a subject. More than one father has said in my counseling office, "I go into my son's room when I get home from work and try to talk to him, but he's unresponsive, so I walk out the door."

"I certainly know what you are talking about," I reply. Then I suggest they find a natural way to spend time in the same room as their teenager for their teenager's benefit. Is it as interesting as something else an adult could be doing? Possibly not. Even if teenagers are not overly responsive, the emotional and relational collateral an adult's presence invests in a young person is immeasurable. We have a limited window to invest ourselves in our teenager's lives. Teens often send the message they are not particularly interested in our company, but I have found the outcome is usually positive if adults remain nearby and open to interaction with them. Obviously, remaining in the vicinity has to have a natural air about it, but it can accomplish the goal of providing some closeness to a teen who is not particularly talkative until the mood strikes. Being nearby can be an asset when a teenager is open to sharing. When sharing occurs, it is wise to remember that adolescents are trying on new ideas for adulthood and we want them to be exploring and sharing their thoughts. We do not have to agree with them yet they need a certain degree of validation for their discoveries and perspectives. These conversations, and other interactions, are more likely to happen when adults are nearby.

Put Me to Bed

Teenagers send the message to caregivers that they want autonomy, but the baby, toddler, young child, and middle-schooler they once were is still inside them. Adolescents—and all the selves within them—need support and love from their caregivers. A national newspaper reported a survey in which 100 children, ages five through eighteen, were asked the question, "What do you most want your parents to know? The first response for more than 90% of the children was "Please do not yell at me. I can't hear you when you yell." The second answer, which included the responses of 16-to-18-year-olds as mentioned, was, "Please put me to bed." Teenagers, like the other children surveyed, long for time to discuss their day with a caring adult when they are transitioning from being busy adolescents into young people going to bed.

I personally have experienced the surprising request to put teenagers to bed. I remember when one of our sons was 15 years old and had entered the phase of initiating very little conversation with me as part of his individuation and separation. My typical overtures to interact with him were met with short, one-word answers throughout the day. Having previously navigated these waters, I knew he was going through the developmental task of getting out of parental gravity. He had barely conversed with me during the previous fourteen hours yet heading up the stairs for bed he said, "Are you coming up?"

"Coming up?" I inquired with genuine curiosity.

"Yeah, to put me to bed," he said, casually.

I felt like saying *I didn't know we still talked to one another*, but replied instead, "Sure, I'll be up in a minute."

Many adolescents would share what is on their minds if adults would be willing to engage with them when teens are open to conversation. Bedtime is one such opportunity. Teens are generally appreciative—even if they don't show it—when adults show some involvement in the long-standing ritual of putting kids to bed.

Brain Change

Discussion about teenagers would not be complete without mentioning the major overhaul happening in their brains. After infancy, the brain's greatest growth spurt occurs in adolescence. These brain-changing forces impact teens' decision-making, which can be overly influenced by emotions, because their brains rely more on the limbic system (the emotional seat of the brain) than the more rational prefrontal cortex. The change in the brain also heightens the importance of connection to a peer group for survival. Humans are dependent on social groups for safety. In adolescence, the primary social group shifts to peers, rather than parents, and membership in the group can feel like a matter of life and death. Also due to brain changes during puberty, the release of dopamine is greater which spurs teenagers toward novelty. Increased dopamine is responsible for the exciting, thrill-seeking behavior evident in many teens and it works to motivate these burgeoning adults toward independence from the family home. Yet depression can ensue as dopamine swings from higher to lower than normal levels. Due to the tremendous changes occurring in this period, the adolescent brain is at a peak for utilizing power and creativity, which pushes teens to think outside the box and try new things. Adolescents in every generation challenge status quo thinking, and influence society with their new values and ideas.

In addition, the changing teen brain considers what has been needed to date and reassigns under-used brain real estate to new purposes. For example, if a young person has not learned secondary languages by puberty, the brain reassigns the language center to new applications, which represent the focus and activities present in the teens' current life. The major overhaul occurring in teenage brains can temporarily impair their effectiveness, like any remodel impairs daily function until it is completed.

FUTURE CASTING

I encourage adults to use something called *future casting* for kids of all ages, which is a positive, realistic forecast of something young people currently may not see for themselves. Realistically forecasting success for kids is a positive addition to improving their confidence and shaping their behavior. It enables them to borrow hope and belief from caregivers about issues they cannot accurately evaluate on their own.

Examples of future casting include *you will make friends at your new school and everyone feels a bit insecure when they are new. It won't take too long for you make good friends.* If this is an informed, realistic concept according to the youngster's tendencies, it will be a boost to their confidence and a reassurance that an important adult forecasts success for them during an insecure time. If this statement does not match their current tendencies, a modified version of this future casting would be *you can learn to make friends and I will help you know how to do it. Everyone can have friends when they know what to do.* This statement would be a great relief to a youngster who is struggling socially.

We assume that young people know their capabilities and positive traits for success, but I suggest that every youngster can benefit from the genuine support and positive reflection back to them about their abilities and their futures. What adults know to be obvious about kids may not be obvious to kids themselves. The words of parents, teachers and other adults help form the psyches of youngsters. Reflecting their positive traits and reminding kids they are capable of achieving the tasks before them are tools which empower young people and train them to have confidence in themselves.

Future casting can also be coupled with discipline or behavior modification as an encouragement that the young person can make the requested corrections. A parent who is annoyed by finding yesterday's food in a lunch box can say, "It's your job to remember to empty your lunch box after school. If you don't, the consequence is _____ and I'm sure you will be able to remember." The repetitive addition of realistic, positive future casting combines discipline with positive faith in the young person, which they cannot help but internalize at some level.

Stating and predicting the good in them can be life changing for young people. I worked with a client who took IQ and aptitude tests as part of an addiction recovery program when he was 51 years old. His IQ was extremely high and the aptitude inventory revealed he was well-suited to being a medical doctor.

Instead, he had lived part of his teenage years and young adulthood on the streets as a drug addict. He left an alcoholic home without finishing high school and sporadically made home repairs to earn money when we he was sober.

He said, "I wish someone would have guided me when I was younger. I had no idea I had the aptitude to go to college and be successful. My parents were divorced and my dad was a drunk. He didn't care if I went to high school. I had no idea that education would have been useful to me."

"What would it have been like if an adult had told you how smart and talented you were, even if you were not making great choices at the time?" I asked.

Tears pooled in his eyes and he said, "It would have made a really big difference. I would not have forgotten words like that even though my life was a mess at the time. I probably would have done something very different with my life eventually."

Words have power and positive, truthful words can linger in the psyche for a lifetime. Children are like wet cement—impressions that are made remain, so why not use the impressionable period of life to accurately state kids' strengths and potential to them?

Future casting is not telling every child they can grow up to be an astronaut or achieve anything they can dream. A few people are gifted enough to achieve almost anything, but most people have a variety of talents and limitations. Future casting is identifying and positively stating for young people the good qualities we observe in them, as well as their potential for success. It applies not only to attributes, but realistic social and vocational outcomes as well as their ability to accomplish the tasks required of them.

DRAWING KIDS CLOSER

It appears to me that our society, which pushes for individual expression, may have forgotten the importance of kids being helped by the connection which exists with adults who care for them. As a society, we may have forgotten that important adults are living templates for what children can become. When things are not going well for a young person, one response is to draw them closer to caring adults, rather than separate and challenge them to

170

figure out on their own how to increase self-control and better their behavior. I am proposing that we draw young people closer as a way to help them emotionally regulate and improve their choices. In addition, drawing kids closer is a component of expressing warmth and appropriate authority as mentioned in Baumrind's blue ribbon quadrant for best parenting practices.

Becca's story illustrates these principles. A single mother brought her 12-year-old daughter Becca into counseling because she was concerned about Becca's friends and their behaviors. Becca's parents were divorced, her father lived several hundred miles away with a new family and Becca had developed a new, questionable social circle in middle school.

One of Becca's new friends stayed at Becca's home on a Friday night. Becca's mother dropped the girls off at a shopping mall on Saturday morning and returned home. After three satisfying hours without interruption, the mother's productive respite was interrupted by a security officer informing her the two girls had been caught shoplifting. The officer asked the mother to come to his office and pick them up. Since it was their first offense, he gave the girls a warning and assured them the police would be contacted if they shoplifted in the store again.

At the end of Becca's individual counseling session with me the following week, the mother asked, "What do I do?!" She was confounded by Becca's choices and frustrated that she had to bear the burden of parenting without support.

"As I understand it," I answered, "Becca generally has good behavior and makes good choices. Is that correct?"

"Basically...," the mother confirmed.

"In this case, I suggest you draw her closer as part of your response. Give her a concrete consequence if you think it is important, but also draw her closer without shaming her. You could say something like, 'I misjudged that you were ready to go to the mall by yourself. Obviously, you're going to keep growing and maturing and you will be able to shop alone someday, but apparently this isn't the right time for you. For now, we'll be together when you shop and we'll spend Saturday mornings together.'"

I made my remarks sound positive, but I knew the implications of my words for Becca's mother. I was suggesting that instead of quiet Saturday mornings like the one she had just relished, Becca's mother should commit more time to her daughter on Saturday mornings to shape Becca's behavior with her own presence. I was proposing she draw Becca closer, rather than deliver a consequence, which meant greater separation between the two of them. My suggestion was not intended to be incarceration for the parent or the child, although I knew in some ways it might feel limiting to Becca's mom who was on the cusp of her own freedom as Becca gained greater independence.

"You don't have to entertain your teenager every Saturday morning," I promised. "Truthfully, she isn't ready to be in the mall without your supervision yet. Take this time to continue building your relationship to her and let her borrow your good judgment until she develops more of it on her own."

"This is a little bit like punishment to me," the mother answered.

"It's a better solution than dealing with the police," I proposed kindly. "And remember, you did not do the shoplifting. I assume you know how to be in a store and not steal merchandise?" I asked humorously.

"Of course I do," the mother answered.

"Then transfer that ability to your daughter through your presence. Create a consequence if you would like to have a punishment for this, but also reel her in closer. She has sent you the message she's not big enough to be out in the world on her own. She will eventually grow up and shop by herself. Until then, increase your presence with her and let her keep learning from you."

I continued seeing Becca for individual counseling regarding the pain she felt about the loss of her father. He had married the woman with whom he had an affair and moved across the country with her children. My young client seldom saw her father. She and her dad were supposed to have telephone conversations at least once a week, but these did not always occur. As independent as Becca occasionally appeared, she was longing for the love and protection of her parents.

In one of our meetings, I casually asked Becca if she had been shopping alone with her friends again. She answered, "No, my mom won't let me. She said I'm not ready to do it yet. Some of my friends go to the mall and each other's houses after school, but I still have to go to the YMCA for after school care."

"What about Saturdays?" I asked.

"Unless I'm at a sleepover or I have something to go to, my mom and I spend Saturday mornings together. I get to sleep in while my mom reads the paper and then we do something like go out to breakfast or make breakfast together at home."

"Is that okay?" I asked.

"Yeah. At first I thought it was a punishment because my mom said we were going to be together on Saturday mornings for the next few months after I got caught shoplifting. But I like it. We get to talk and laugh together more. She said I can shop alone with friends when I'm older," Becca answered.

"What about your friend who also got caught shoplifting? Do you still get to spend time with her?" I asked.

"Yeah," Becca replied, "she's one of my friends, but I do stuff with other friends too. One time she stayed over on Friday night and my mom took us both to the mall and we shopped together. It was okay."

I gleaned from the client's remarks that her mother had followed my suggestion and limited her daughter's freedom until she had further maturity. The young client did not appear to be suffering under her mother's restriction and I sensed a greater degree of connection had occurred in their relationship. Becca initially resisted the idea of her mother's increased control and presence, but there appeared to be something positive in the extra time spent with her mom.

I was confident Becca was a normal, developing teenager who would mature with time and that her mother was a sensible, dedicated mom who was doing a good job of single parenting. By drawing her daughter closer, the mother was able to lend Becca more parental presence and self-control while the opportunity was still available to both of them. They actually flourished in it. Becca reported that her increased time with her mother was a positive time in her week.

Teenagers seldom ask for more closeness when they are in the developmental stage of separation from their parents. Yet they benefit from increased parental presence when their drive for individuation gets ahead of good judgment. All caregivers experience pressure from teens to give them freedom—to let them be who they are because they are different than their parents—and teens believe they have informed, or even better perspectives for living in the world than their parents do. Adults generally want to see young people develop into their full selves, but when autonomy gets ahead of positive outcomes, it is a signal that young people need more grounding in the company of adults who care for them.

Reeling children closer when they are not doing well does not exclude also giving them consequences for bad behavior. Some misbehavior needs concrete consequences as a deterrent to help kids learn to make better choices. Drawing young people closer at the same time gives them an additional source of strength for retooling their behavior. When these two approaches go hand in hand, young people have a stronger framework for internalizing the changes they need to make. Young people may not ask for more time with their parents, but they benefit when parents are present and available to kids.

Some parents might consider it a counter-intuitive step to increase their presence when young people are making poor choices yet emotional and social relationships are the environment in which young people learn to function within their societies. Increasing presence does not imply that a parent condones inappropriate behavior. Instead, gathering children closer sends the message that a young person will receive support and further instruction for getting their behavior right alongside someone who has greater maturity. This response can enable youngsters to be more successful when they are struggling to make right choices with their immature brains.

TIME IN VS. TIME OUT

Time Out is a common disciplinary strategy parents use as a consequence for their children's unacceptable behaviors. Time Out requires kids to individually calm down and regain their composure. It means separation from others. At times, it can be the right solution to a problem.

A book titled *Time In: When Time Out Doesn't Work* advocates for structured time spent with children by engaging them with questions, requiring them to attend to themselves and others, and to make amends when needed. It is a behavior-shaping modality for youngsters at home and school.

I use the phrase Time In in a different way, as an in-the-moment version of drawing young people closer. The action I refer to as Time In is simply bringing kids closer physically and lending them an adult's emotional regulation when they are struggling to find it within themselves. Caregivers regularly transfer what is inside themselves to the kids in their care. Time In is the intentional transfer of emotional regulation to kids who need help because they cannot find their own way to play cooperatively or be aware of others. It is non-punitive and can be used as a direct response to wrong behavior.

Rather than separate a child from a group, playmate, or sibling as punishment for uncooperative play, Time In is the consequence of requiring the child to sit in the parent's lap, or next to a caregiving adult, who waits with them for a short period of time. It does not involve reading a story or any other form of entertainment—it is just an opportunity to help calm a youngster with an adult's physical presence for a brief period of time. It can take place right where a problem is occurring. It can be used with toddlers through teenagers. The intent of Time In is to be encouraging and non-shaming, with the promise that the young person can re-join the play after they have spent time in the adult's loving presence. It is a good parental response for sibling rivalry and conflict among young people.

The mother of twin girls said Time In was a very useful strategy at her house when her children were three to fourteen years old. She said her daughters were quite close to each other and generally played together well. Yet like all children, they had differences of opinion and sometimes fought over toys or who chose the direction for their play. The mother said Time In was a relief to her because it meant she could intervene if necessary, but not referee her daughters' fights. Instead, if the girls were struggling too long with their arguments, she proposed that they both had Time In with her, after which they could figure out how they wanted to play together. Sometimes 'threatening' Time In was sufficient to remind them they should find agreement between themselves before they had to take a break with their mom. At other times during Time In, they snuggled on the couch together for a few minutes in lieu of arguing, which helped them re-group and go back to successful play. She said, "It never seems like a punishment to the girls when I give them Time In. If I do give them Time In, it helps them calm down and change their dynamics." Then she added, "Plus, I offer it when they have friends over if they're fighting for a friend's attention. When the interaction between the girls becomes too competitive, I suggest Time In and they figure something out right away, rather than leave their friend and sit on my lap. It's been really useful. It's better than a punishment or listening to the girls fight."

Time In is not intended as punishment, although generally kids would rather play than sit quietly with a parent. Time In is a brief respite from negative interactions which can be calmed by connection with an adult. Although it is not entertainment, Time In should generally be a positive experience. It appealed to a friend one afternoon when our two boys were having conflict while a playmate was visiting. I eventually responded and asked, "Do you guys need Time In?"

The visiting friend inquired what Time In meant and the boys explained. Our sons both declined because they wanted to keep playing, but the visiting friend enthusiastically said, "I would!"

The youngster sat with me for a little while and I gave him kind attention. After a few minutes, he said, "I'm ready to go back and play," to which I responded, "Okay, Time In is over." He returned to playing with the boys, after which they were quite cooperative with each other.

A father of four children told me their oldest son often became restless at the dinner table and Time In after dinner settled him before the evening started. Their few minutes together refilled the son's heart and enabled him to be non-competitive with his younger siblings who needed his parent's focus after dinner with baths, pajamas and bedtime stories. The needs of older children can get lost in the many demands of younger siblings. In this case, the father discovered a few minutes of Time In af-

ter dinner set the stage for his oldest son to have more cooperative evenings before his own bedtime. The father was sending the
message through his presence that the oldest son mattered to him.
Everyone benefits when love is present.

I observe a troubling trend toward disconnection between
parents and children. The abundant use of electronic devices is
one component which increases the separateness of people who
live together. We are at a time in history where external stimuli
impact our daily lives at an unprecedented level. Humans continue to share living space as they have for generations, but the
connection and time spent interacting among them is decreasing.

A physician and colleague noted he has seen a significant
rise in childhood anxiety over the last decade. He says it is the
predominant presenting issue for young people who come to his
office, eclipsing illness and ADHD as parental concerns. The increased use of electronic devices parallels this trajectory during
the same the decade. I personally believe these two trends are
interconnected. Our society has seen a significant decrease in
interpersonal connection, due in part to the increase of electron-
ics, which may play a part in increased anxiety. Increasing the
time family members interact with and spend time together could
be vital to the health and well-being of our young people. The
fact that Time In is effective in helping kids calm down may be
evidence that separation increases anxiety for young people. It is
wise for us to look at the correlation between these two variables
in parenting the next generation.

Time In does not reward bad behavior, nor is it the only response for helping young people act responsibly. Time In is not
solely sufficient for disciplining kids who need direct and clear
consequences for their wrong actions. Young people of all ages
need limits, and caregivers are the source of authority to reinforce
behavioral requirements. Time In is not permissive parenting. Instead, it is the powerful intervention of an adult's positive presence transferred to kids.

TOOLS FOR CONVERSATIONS WITH KIDS

A question I am often asked is "How do I tell my son or
daughter about ____?" Seldom is this question about how to have
fun or share something exciting because adults usually know how

to give good news to their kids. Instead, caregivers want ideas for telling their family members about divorces, moves, and other difficult topics. The following strategies are ideas for giving information to young people they might not be happy to hear or when difficult questions have to be answered.

For example, a divorced parent asked, "How do I answer my daughter's questions about her dad's love?" The mother reported that the child's father had recently moved into the home of his new girlfriend and her two children. The daughter had spent very little time with her dad since the divorce, and the daughter was experiencing more competition for her father's time since he had become part of a new family. The ten-year-old girl saw her own therapist who recommended the girl be told that her dad loved her very much and he would not love her any less because he had a new family.

But is it true? I wondered. I believe people can metabolize the truth, even if it is painful, but they cannot fully digest something which is not true, even if they want to believe it. Non-truth simply does not make its way through all of our mental, emotional and intuitive human filters. Therefore, I disagreed with the therapist of my client's daughter. I said, "I don't recommend you hurt your daughter unnecessarily by telling her something painful, but I also find that youngsters cannot metabolize statements that are not true. Unless your ex-husband loves her very much she won't be able to accept what you're saying. Is it true?" I asked. "Does your ex-husband love his daughter a great deal?"

"Not in a way that is obvious to me," the client answered. "When she was young, her dad asked me to keep her even on his weekends. As she grew older, he came to her soccer games, but he did not actually want to spend time with her. He's a really selfish guy."

"Why does your daughter's therapist believe he loves her as much as she suggests?" I inquired.

"I don't know," the client answered. "She thinks it's important to reframe what my daughter thinks into something positive. My daughter was telling the counselor that it seems like her dad is more interested in his girlfriend's kids than her."

"Is that true?" I asked.

"Basically, yes" she answered.

"Then your daughter won't be able to believe it," I replied. "Or she will get confused about how love acts and feels and she'll come to think this is the right way to be loved by important people."

"What should I tell her instead?" my client asked.

"An appropriate, non-hurtful version of the truth if you can," I suggested. I proposed an answer such as, "People love in different ways and I can't say exactly how much your dad loves you, but I know you are lovable and you deserve to be loved. It's hard to have him spend more time with the other kids and I know you love your dad. I wish you could experience more of his love."

I recommended not criticizing the child's father in the process and I encouraged her to keep the focus on the truth that her daughter is worthy of love in all circumstances, whether or not her father is giving her the attention she seeks. I reminded my client that children see the world with themselves at the center and her daughter was using her dad as a feedback loop of her lovability and worth. I encouraged my client to help her daughter process her feelings about her dad's new family and to validate the child's experience, but to focus on the helpful, digestible truth that the daughter is lovable, it feels bad to have your dad give his attention elsewhere and her dad is missing out on knowing an awesome person. I also suggested she validate that it's normal to want your dad's love and attention—organically that is how life is supposed to be. Each of these statements are true, which kids can accept on an organic level.

Answering Kids Questions

Much has already been said about giving kids appropriate truth. There is a sweet spot in speaking the truth with young people because kids need enough correct information to make sense of their experiences and not too much information to make life unnecessarily hard for them. Young people facing difficult circumstances will be better prepared if they are given an appropriate amount of information about what lies ahead. Telling the truth can often be accomplished without unnecessarily hurting them.

In the client's case above, it would have been very painful for a child to ask how much her father loved her and have the mother reply, "Clearly, not much! He doesn't want to spend any time with you." In truth, the child's mother did not know how much her ex-husband loved their daughter. She would have had to ask him in order to give an accurate report to their child, which is not the ultimate purpose of her question. The girl was hurt, which brought up questions about her worth. The father is responsible to communicate to his daughter how much he loves and values her with congruent words and behaviors. In the meantime, the mother can give an honest and least hurtful response to the daughter to help her understand the situation. A loving adult can consider the real intent behind a young person's question and give enough truthful information to help them digest what is happening and prepare for what may happen in the future.

Trust

Speaking truth appropriately creates trust and safety for others. Children are completely dependent on adults and the only way they can feel safe is to trust the adults who care for them, which includes giving kids correct, appropriate answers as needed. Adults who can be trusted have young people's best interests at heart when responding to their questions.

Trust is derived from dependability. Sometimes in order to be trustworthy, adults have to express truth to others, which may be painful for them to hear. Speaking difficult truth to kids with sensitivity equips them to face their circumstances. There are times when all of us need to hear something we would prefer not to hear, such as a job is ending, a best friend is moving, or a medical diagnosis is more serious than we had hoped. Kids face similar challenges and their reactions are no less important. For example, adults may have a straightforward understanding about a move which means more income for the family and better schools, but kids may find the same news devastating. They may be strongly attached to friends and activities in their current community, therefore, the promise of something better does not outweigh the pain of losing something important. As hard as it may be to field a young person's emotional reaction to bad news, protecting them from the truth unnecessarily can contribute to greater distress and an inability to cope without preparation.

Sharing Difficult Truth

Caregivers need to be honest with themselves when they decide to give difficult information to young people. Are they spilling truth onto kids because they are careless, have no other place to share it, or because they want to wound someone in return for hurting them? Telling children bad news because it creates relief for a parent is a wrong motive for sharing with kids.

Keeping in mind the best interests of the listener requires that adult caregivers consider what it will be like for a young person to hear difficult information. Will it prepare them for something hard or will it unnecessarily worry them in situations where they will be only minimally impacted? Dropping painful information on kids without the appropriate environment, time and opportunity for hearing their response is a disservice to them. For example, the first day of college is not the best time to tell teenagers their parents are planning to divorce. Ideally, the first day of college should be focused on the needs of the new college student, and the conversation about divorce should wait until the student is in a position to share their reaction.

As discussed, most kids hear about a situation from the viewpoint *What does this mean for me? Who am I because of it?* The following are tools for sharing information with youngsters of all ages.

Give Some Warning

As part of his mystique and escapism arts, the great Harry Houdini invited people to strike him full force in his stomach. He received thousands of blows to his abdomen as he traveled the world. Ironically, a blow to the stomach also ended Houdini's life. The fateful event occurred when a contender positioned himself in front of the Great Houdini and punched him in the gut before Houdini constricted his stomach muscles. The lack of protection from taut muscles enabled the blow to penetrate and Houdini died from injuries to his midsection, even though he had survived thousands of previous punches.

Bad news can feel like a punch in the gut. Giving people a chance to prepare for the blow helps them handle the information. A preparatory, warning statement can be gentle and subtle. Prefacing a difficult conversation can be as simple as, "I have to tell you something you don't want to hear...," or, "I know you were excited about the idea of going on a road trip with your friends, but you are not going to like my answer..." Each of these introductions gives a young person the opportunity to metaphorically tighten their stomach muscles to withstand an undesirable blow. Prepping kids about less than desirable news reflects a degree of attunement to them. Other examples of preparatory statements are:

> "I wish I could say yes, but...,"
> "You're not going to like what I'm about to say...,"
> "Something unfortunate happened today and I
> need to tell you about it...,"
> "You're going to have an opportunity to grow from
> this problem..."

For most of us bad news is still bad news, but its form of delivery can lessen or increase the impact of the blow. Medical patients often speak of the way doctors delivered news to them about unwelcome diagnoses. Parents, like doctors, can be mindful of the style they use to deliver unhappy information. One way to slide into a difficult conversation is with a preparatory introduction.

Playing Their Card First

Stating another person's objections before information is shared can reduce the conflictual nature of an exchange. This strategy names the other person's position first and shows awareness for their perspective. In the case of parents and teenagers, playing their card first would be something like, "You're probably going to think I don't understand. I know you're a good driver and you haven't had an accident, but I'm not going to let you take my car on a road trip." A teenager can argue the unreasonable nature of a parent's answer, but there are few unmentioned counter arguments left for the teen when a caregiver has already mentioned the teen's objections first. As disappointed as a teen may be, when parents mention the teen's perspectives first they are reflecting knowledge of the problem from the teen's viewpoint. Everyone seeks to be understood and this tactic can provide understanding as well as aid in the delivery of unhappy news. It can reduce conflict with peers, partners and young people because the first line of communication states *I understand your position is this...* followed by a message.

Grownups are Going to Handle This

This topic has been covered in the first section of the book, but it is so important from a young person's perspective it deserves mentioning again as part of conversations with kids. Children are faced with problems over which they have no control. Situations arise which directly affect young people and they usually have no ability to make things better. Giving youngsters assurance that the adults in their lives will work to solve a problem, which really is a grownup problem, gives kids tremendous relief. Adults caring for children usually know that a problem is outside the realm for young people to solve, but they seldom state this. Kids worry and work hard to solve problems they have no power to solve, until someone frees them from the burden by stating what is in the realm of young people to resolve and what will be handled by adults.

Earning money, providing food, auto repairs, getting jobs, caring for young children, safety, and other essentials are grownup responsibilities. Yet young people carry the burden of trying to handle these responsibilities until adults communicate that they can be trusted to meet children's needs. Sometimes the statement, "This is a grownup problem and grownups are going to handle it," is sufficient for relieving the stress kids carry.

Another form of kids taking too much responsibility for problems is apparent in youngsters who come to my office for counseling as victims of sexual abuse. Invariably, young people take some degree of responsibility for their sexual violation. They have no idea that culpability rests anywhere, but with them, until I mention, "This is a grownup problem and grownups are going to take care of it." Kids of all ages are changed by these remarks. Their bodies soften, they exhale and they begin to release the tension they have been carrying from a situation that is out of their control. My statement is not the complete and final resolution to their problems, but shifting responsibility for the situation to adults frees young people who may have assumed they were responsible for unwanted sexual touch.

Appropriately saying to young people, "Grownups are going to handle this," or in the case of teenagers, "We're going to help you solve this problem," are important statements for keeping a problem and the power to solve it in the right hands. Seldom is the power to solve big problems in the hands of young people. Youngsters need to be relieved from responsibility in situations over which they genuinely have no control. Once again, it is not uncommon for adults to assume children think like adults think. In order for youngsters to think correctly, caregivers need to give them the information that grownups will be handling certain problems, without assuming kids already have this perspective. Probably five out of 100 kids have replied, "I know," when I have told them, "This is a grownup problem and grownups are going to take care of it." The other 95 or so are relieved by the information. Without such knowledge, youngsters make up their own ideas and carry responsibility, which caregivers have no idea they are carrying.

Taking Responsibility for a Time to Talk

When dealing with a difficult situation or delivering bad news to kids, adults can take responsibility for making sure young people have time to ask questions and discuss the problems in the present and future. Dropping information with the phrase, "We can talk about this later," does not necessarily mean a productive conversation will follow unless an adult takes responsibility for it. Attunement to kids in such a case means paying attention to what young people need and understanding that they will have many reactions. Proposing a specific time to circle back and re-open dialogue is an aspect of attunement. An adult taking responsibility for a later conversation is the strategic tool suggested here.

Setting a follow up time can be a hard strategy for caregivers because it is not easy to deliver disappointing news and then intentionally re-engage it. Yet for young people, an adult circling back means the young person's inner world matters and they will have a definite time to express their reactions. The tactic of suggesting a specific, later time keeps communication open as much as possible between kids and caregivers. Proposing a later conversation—and following through on it—circumvents angry, below-the-surface emotions in kids. Adult initiation on the front end can mean less turmoil on the back end of problems.

Not all situations require a later appointment for conversation, but some difficult subjects require many discussions. It really does make a difference if a caregiver says, "We can talk more about this and I will bring it up," rather than, "Let me know if you have anything else you want to say about this." Evidence suggests an open door policy in business is less successful than scheduled times for discussion and planning. The same is true in families.

Many situations, especially difficult ones, cannot be discussed in one sitting. Intentionally creating opportunities for youngsters to share their thoughts and concerns over the course of a problem, and genuinely listening to their experiences, sets them up for greater cooperation and leaves them with an understanding that although things may not go their way, others care about how they are doing. The idea *if a child had a problem they would tell me* is erroneous. Young people usually attempt to communicate what is bothering them. If adults are not paying attention, the messages may go underground and emerge as non-verbal communication and sometimes as difficult behavior. Taking the lead to help young people process what is happening to and around them can be overlooked in parenting. If you were to ask a child, "Do you want me to bring this up, or will you bring it up when you're ready?" I venture most kids would prefer to have adults initiate conversations.

Section Two
Summary

The ideas mentioned in this chapter reflect common, repeated conversations I have had with many parents and other caregivers. I find myself sharing the same ideas with many adults because young people have similar problems, and some of these problems can be addressed with common strategic tools. Helping kids discover and implement strategies for successful living is a component of good parenting.

In summary, research has shown that an optimum amount of adult responsiveness and requiring makes for the best outcomes in parenting. Extremes on either of these two axes hurt kids more than helps them. Caregivers who desire to equip young people with skills for life need to require culturally appropriate behaviors from them and respond with positivity and warmth. These two elements—requiring and responding—form the components that make young people successful in self-management and cooperation with others. Responding includes *please don't yell at me* and *put me to bed.*

Another strategic tool is to teach young people how to fill their hearts with universal love, which is available to them at all times. In our current culture, young people spend less time with their families and significantly more time with devices which cannot love or reflect value back to them. A universal source is always available to fill their hearts with love.

Young people flourish from validation, which is understanding the world from their perspectives and reflecting their perspectives back to them. Kids needs validation that their worth, needs, and ideas are recognized by important adults.

Social aptitude can be a better predictor of success than intelligence and not all kids know it is paramount for them to learn emotional self-regulation, have awareness of others, and generate ideas that consider themselves and others. Adults who want to help kids can teach them these very specific behaviors, which are the universal components of positive social relationships.

Drawing kids closer and Time In versus Time Out are alternative methods for helping young people down regulate their emotions and become centered in appropriate behavior. These concepts speak to an aspect of parenting wherein adults transfer to youngsters the ability to calm, be less reactive, and think through responses that may be more effective than kids' initial reactions to their circumstance.

Tools for conversations with young people have been presented. These ideas include stating a young person's position first, prepping them to receive bad news, assuring them that grownups are going to solve certain problems and taking responsibility for a time to talk. It's erroneous to assume that kids will circle back to complete unfinished conversations, so adults can assure young people that they will move an unresolved problem to completion.

Finally, future casting has been discussed as a powerful way to predict positive outcomes for young people who cannot always see their gifts and potential for success. Positive traits and the likelihood of success may be obvious to parents and teachers, but that does not mean young children, insecure teenagers and late adolescents know who they are and what they can be in the world. Stating these truths, even when they might seem unbelievable to the young person, is a foundation adults can offer to make kids' lives better.

All of these ideas portray the truth that young people need adults all the way into their own adulthood. Grownups matter to youngsters, sometimes more than adults can imagine. Parents and primary caregivers are the first life skills manual kids use to navigate the world. The ideas, expectations and behaviors communicated from adults to kids become a working life map that guides young people for the rest of life. There are ways to make positive and negative contributions to a young person's life manual. The suggestions offered here are road-tested, positive responses adults can use to equip kids to be the best versions of themselves in the present and the future.

Chapter Nine

Conclusion

The message of this book could be summed up in the following story. During a Lifespan Integration session, an adult client spontaneously said, "I made a mistake. I thought I was unlovable." We were targeting a very young memory and he tenderly shared the insight, which emerged during the process. He was accessing very young ways of thinking that were held in the neural networks of his body. His erroneous thinking became apparent and the client said with new awareness, "I thought I was worthless, but I was a normal child. I needed people to love me and my parents didn't know how to connect. It wasn't about me at all!"

I confirmed his new awareness. "No child is unlovable," I said. "No one comes into the world as a worthless human being. You came up with the wrong conclusion."

The client explained that his parents were poorly skilled in relating to him as a child and as an adult. "They were quite detached throughout my life," he said. "I just assumed it was something wrong with me." His life could have been quite different if he had understood earlier that he was a valuable person whose parents were quite limited.

This client's story has been repeated in my office many, many times. People establish inaccurate ways of thinking in the early years of their lives, and their erroneous thinking lasts for decades. Young clients spontaneously mention they are bad because bad things happened to them, they were yelled at, or they miscomprehended situations. I heard their stories often enough that I felt moved to address a greater audience and share what kids were telling me. In so many ways, they were completely incorrect, but life did not auto-correct their beliefs. I found it took intentional effort, and sometimes professional therapy, to help young people find the truth about themselves, others and life. Every day, I see clients change their deep internal beliefs and live better lives as a result from upgrading their thinking.

My hope for sharing the ideas about what young people think is threefold:

First, I hope parents, teachers, caregivers, coaches, doctors, family members and all those who interface with young people will understand that kids do not think as we assume they do. They do not think like adults. Youngsters think very differently in the circumstances they share with grownups and what kids believe can be unbelievable. I want adults to know the importance of discovering what toddlers through late adolescents think about themselves, others and the world. The only way we will know what kids think is to ask them. Young people commonly generate ideas we cannot imagine as the stories in this text portray. Adults are in a position to correct kids' thinking before decades of erroneous *I am* beliefs and hurtful strategies become established ways of living. When adults know what young people believe, parents and caregivers can help them correct erroneous thinking and live different lives.

Second, I hope it is evident to adults that young people from very young children to burgeoning adults arrive at wrong beliefs innocently. Intelligence and optimum parenting do not create immunity from wrong thinking. Erroneous ways of thinking occur around the globe in every strata of life. Kids use their young minds to understand circumstances in ways adults cannot imagine because kids are neophytes in the world. They do not know what grownups know until adults help them understand themselves and their situations correctly. Children do not set out to have outrageous ideas; they acquire wrong thinking honestly as they make their way through life.

Third, young people achieve very different outcomes when they make decisions based on truth instead of their young, uninformed beliefs. What children think—especially about themselves —influences their behavior, choice of friends, success in school and ultimately every one of their relationships. If kids determine they are good and likable, they interface with the world expecting good outcomes and consider the negative bumps along the way as obstacles to be overcome. Their resilience emerges time and again. If young people believe they are bad, they withdraw, misbehave and hurt others. Negative beliefs about themselves lead to negative perceptions about others, and less than ideal outcomes repeat in their lives. When we see troubled children, we can be certain they have negative beliefs about themselves and others. The opposite is also true. Accurate, positive thinking leads to positive behavior and expectations.

The ways young people develop their thinking has been presented, which includes that young people perceive the world with themselves at the center and use cause-and-effect thinking to understand their worlds. It is not uncommon for young people to assume something personal about external events. In many cases, kids believe something they have done or said has caused what is happening around them. Young people take words at face value and believe what they are told. Young children believe cultural myths and most youngsters believe some aspects of what adults tell them about their worth, capabilities and their futures. Young people are prone to form *I am* beliefs as a result of their experiences and these beliefs influence their lives. Kids of all ages use what happens around them, to them, and within them to develop constructs about their personal value. This experiential data converts into *I am* beliefs that become embedded in young people's neural networks and affects the rest of their lives. Young people develop strategies in response to their situations and these strategies become life-long patterns. Kids interact with their environments and adjust according to what they encounter. Their adaptive behaviors become methods for coping with life and last well beyond the timeframe in which their strategies developed.

The ideas presented throughout the text are important because current culture evidences some challenging trends. Unfortunately, more youngsters are diagnosed with depression and anxiety than ever before. Depression, in part, is about negative beliefs which can be corrected. Anxiety contains suppressed feelings which can be metabolized within caring family groups when adult connection and care are present.

In addition, parenting expectations shift every half decade or so. In the face of these ever-changing expectations, there are core concepts for raising young people which transcend time and culture.

All of the categories mentioned here are derived from one foundational point—children live what they believe. The ways young people interpret what they experience about themselves and others, combined with their natural temperaments, become templates for living. Therefore, it is important to know what kids are thinking in order to understand their feelings and actions.

In many cases it is possible to influence erroneous thinking once it has been discovered. Sometimes intercepting the way young people perceive circumstances requires professional therapies that can access the misperceptions and old feelings held in the body. Other times, caregivers can use their adult insight and other strategies to help young people think correctly.

Why is this important? Because *you won't believe what your child is thinking.*

Notes

Chapter 1
Fogel summarizes the essence of Fogel, Steven Jay. *Your Mind Is What Your Brain Does for a Living.* Austin, Texas. 2014. Michael Oher's story is a Oher, Michael. I Beat the Odds from Homelessness, to the Blind Side, and Beyond. New York. 2011.

Chapter 2
Light can be measured as Quantum Mystery of Light Revealed by New Experiment—Live Science https://www.livescience.com. Strange News, Nov 5, 2012.

Chapter 3
The brain uses the degree Cozolina, Louis, The Neuroscience of Psychotherapy – Healing the Social Brain. New York.2002.

Chapter 4
Tom Hilton, a colleague, Interview. Minneapolis, MN 2017. *Teens are growing rapidly and* Siegel, Daniel Brainstorm: The Power and Purpose of the Teenage Brain. New York. 2013.

Chapter 5
People receive data from their Cooper, Robert K, The Other 90%. New York. 2002. *Elaine Aaron in her book* Aron, Elaine N. The Undervalued Self. New York. 2010. *Adults can underestimate the impact of* Seigal 2015; *Michelle Beaudreau, a school counselor* interview 2016; *The most common childhood traumas* Fogel, 2014: Fear, anxiety, and worry stem Reinecke, 2010.

Chapter 6
Individuals who experienced the events Thorpe, Catherine, The Success and Strategies of Lifespan Integration. WA. 2012; *The most common childhood traumas* Robin L. Kay, Ph.D Los Angeles, CA 2012...*a parent, an older sibling* Fogel, Steven Jay. Your Mind is What Your Brain Does for a Living. Texas, 2014.

Chapter 7

Babies are most often in Lipton, Bruce 2008; *Cooper offers another way to* Cooper, Robert K, The Other 90% 2002., *For example, the toilet training,* Azrin, Natan and Foxx Richard (1974) Toilet Training in Less Than A Day; Pocket Books, Division of Simon & Schuster, New York, 1969. *Lipton writes: By the time* Lipton, Bruce The Biology of Belief. USA.2008; *Cooper offers another way to* Cooper, Robert K, The Other 90% 2002., *Siegel writes that the mind* Siegel, Daniel The Developing Mind: How Relationships and the Brain Interact to Shape Who We Are, Second Edition. New York. 2012.

Chapter 8

In 1943, Abraham Maslow presented Cherry (2014) What Is Maslow's Hierarchy of Needs? www.verywell.com › Living Well › Psychology › Theories of Personality Development. *Experts report that mental and* Siegel, Daniel (2012) *The Developing Mind: How Relationships and the Brain Interact to Shape Who We Are,* Second Edition. New York; Sibcy, Clinton and Hawkins, 2015. *Researchers have learned that the* Goleman, Daniel Emotional Intelligence; *Why it Can Matter More than IQ.* Bantam Books, New York 2006. *The ability to maintain a* Goleman, omit , Daniel (2006) *Emotional Intelligence; Why it Can Matter More than IQ.* Bantam Books, New York. *Educators find that children with* Ricci, Mary Kay, *Mindsets in the Classroom: building a culture of success and achievement in schools.* Texas 2013 . *Dweck, author of the culture-changing* Dweck, Carol (2008) *Mindset: The New Psychology of Success.* New York. *Dr. Robert Cloninger at Washington* Bronson, Po and Merryman, Ashley (2009) *Nurture Shock, New Thinking About Children.* New York. *Dweck and others found that* Dweck, Carol (2008) *Mindset: The New Psychology of Success.* New York. *A resource I recommend for* Janis-Norton, Noel (2013) *Calmer, Easier, Happier Parenting – Five Strategies That End the Daily Battles and Get Kids to Listen the First Time.* USA. *In a very well-known and* Baumrind, Diana *Effects of Authoritative Parental Control on Child Behavior and Development.* Child Development 37 (4) 1966.

Chapter 9
Hall and Cook wrote a Hall, Karyn and Cook, Melissa. *The Power of Validation: Arming Your Child against Bullying, Peer Pressure, Addiction, Self-Harm and Out-of-Control Emotions.* Oakland, CA 2012. *According to Marano, a simple* Marano, Hara Estroff, *"Why Doesn't Anybody Like Me?" A Guide to Raising Socially Confident Kids.* New York. *Studies indicate a strong parallel* Marano, Hara Estroff (1998) *"Why Doesn't Anybody Like Me?" A Guide to Raising Socially Confident Kids.* New York. *A national newspaper reported a* Seattle Times, 2015. *Maccoby and Martin added a* Maccoby, E. E., Martin, J. A. Socialization in the context of the family: Parent-child interaction. In P. H. Mussen (Ed.), Handbook of child psychology (1983). *Discussion about teenagers would not* Siegel, Daniel Brainstorm: *The Power and Purpose of the Teenage Brain.* New York. 2013. *A book titled Time In:* Jean Islley Clark, *Time In: When Time-Out Doesn't Work,* Chicago, Il 1999. *A physician and colleague noted* Interview, Edward W. Freedman, MD. Bellevue WA. 2018.

References

Ackerman, Paul (1980). Signals: *What Your Child is Trying to Tell You.* New York: Signet.

Al-Chalabi, A., Turner, M. Delamont, R. S. (2010). *The Brain: A Beginner's Guide.* Oxford, England: One World Publications.

Aron, Elaine N. (2010). *The Undervalued Self: Restore Your Love/Power Balance, Transform the Inner Voice That Holds You Back, and Find Your True Self-Worth.* New York: Little, Brown and Company.

Azrin, Natan and Foxx, Richard (1974). *Toilet Training in Less Than A Day.* New York: Pocket Books, Division of Simon & Schuster.

Baumrind, Diana (1966). *Effects of Authoritative Parental Control on Child Behavior and Development.* Child Development 37 (4) pp. 887-907.

Baumrind, Diana (1967). *Child care practices anteceding three patterns of preschool behavior.* Genetic Psychology Monographs. 75 (1), 43-88.

Blankenship, Donna Gordon (July 13, 2014). *No gadgets required: Parents' talking aids baby brain growth.* The Seattle Times.

Boudreau, Michelle. *Personal communication.*

Bronson, Po and Merryman, Ashley (2009). *Nurtureshock: New Thinking About Children.* New York: Twelve, Hachette Book Group.

Carlson, Richard (1997). *You Can Be Happy No Matter What; Five Principles Your Therapist Never Told You.* Novata, CA: New World Library.

Cherry, Kendra_(May 16, 2017). 'The Five Levels of Maslow's Hierarchy of Needs' retrieved from https://www.verywell.com/maslows-needs-hierarchy-2795961

Cooper, Robert K. (2002). *The Other 90%.* New York: Penguin Random House.

Dweck, Carol (2008). *Mindset: The New Psychology of Success.* New York: Penguin Random House.

Duke, Patty (March 6, 2014). 'Compassion and hope for parents who abuse their children.' The Seattle Times, p. A11.

Feinstein, Sheryl (2009). *Inside the Teenage Brain: Parenting a Work in Progress.* Plymouth, UK: Rowman and Littlefield.

Fogel, Steven Jay (2014). *Your Mind is What Your Brain Does for a Living.* Austin, Texas: Greenleaf Group Book Press.

Goleman, Daniel, (2006). *Emotional Intelligence: Why It Can Matter More than IQ.* New York: Bantam Books.

Grout, Pam (2014). *E-cubed: Nine More Energy Experiments That Prove Manifesting Magic and Miracles Is Your Full-Time Gig.* Carlsbad, CA: Hay House.

Hall, Karyn and Cook, Melissa (2012). *The Power of Validation: Arming Your Child against Bullying, Peer Pressure, Addiction, Self-Harm and Out-of-Control Emotions.* Oakland, CA.

Hilton, Tom (2015). 'Interview Minneapolis,' MN.

Janis-Norton, Noel (2013). *Calmer, easier, happier parenting: Five strategies that end the daily battles and get kids to listen the first time.* New York: The Penguin Group.

Keller, Helen (1996). *The Story of My Life.* New York: Dover Publications.

Lipton, Bruce (2008). *The Biology of Belief: Unleashing the Power of Consciousness, Matter, & Miracles.* Carlsbad, CA: Hay House.

Lowen, Alexander (1995). *Narcissim: Denial of the True Self.* New York: Simon and Schuster.

Maccoby, Eleanor E. (Nov., 1992). *The role of parents in the socialization of children: An historical overview. Developmental Psychology,* Vol 28(6), 1006-1017.

Maccoby and Martin (1983). *Handbook of Child Psychology.*

Marano, Hara Estroff (1998). *"Why Doesn't Anybody Like Me?" A Guide to Raising Socially Confident Kids.* New York: William Morrow and Company.

McLaren, Karla (2010). *The Language of Emotions: What Your Feelings are Trying to Tell You.* Boulder, CO: Sounds True, Inc.

Mowe, Sam (July / August, 2014). Q&A with Dr. Dan Siegel. Spirituality & Health' Volume 17, number 4

Neel Burton (May 23, 2012). 'Our Hierarchy of Needs Why true freedom is a luxury of the mind.' Retrieved from https://www.psychologytoday.com/blog/hide-and-seek/201205/our-hierarchy-needs

Oher, Michael (2011). *I Beat the Odds from Homelessness, to the Blind Side, and Beyond.* New York, USA: Gotham Books.

Ortland, Anne (2002). *Children are Wet Cement.* Lincoln, NE: iUniverse.

Pace, Peggy (2009), *Lifespan Integration: Connecting Ego States Through Time.* Snoqualmie, WA: Author.

Reinecke, Mark A. (2010). *Little Ways to Keep Calm and Carry On.* Oakland, CA: New Harbinger Publications, Inc.

Ricci, Mary Kay, (2013) *Mindsets in the classroom: Building a culture of success and achievement in schools.* Waco, Texas: Prufrock Press Inc.

Robin Nixon (July 8, 2012). 'Adolescent Angst: 5 Facts About the Teen Brain.' Retrieved from https://www.livescience.com/21461-teen-brain-adolescence-facts.html

Row, Claudia, (May 15, 2015). 'Teachers learn to get at root of bad behavior. 'The Seattle Times, p. 1.

Russel, Mark (2013). 'Brain Evolution, Neurobiology and EMDR.' (Lecture). Amen Clinic, WA.

Seligman, Martin, (2007). *The Optimistic Child: A Proven Program to Safeguard Children Against Depression and Build Lifelong Resilience.* New York: Houghton Mifflin Harcourt Publishing Company.

Siegel, Daniel (2010). *Mindsight. The New Science of Personal Transformation.* New York: Random House Publishing Group..

Siegel, Daniel (2012). *The Developing Mind: How Relationships and the Brain Interact to Shape Who We Are* (2nd Ed.) New York: The Guilford Press.

Siegel, Daniel (2013). *Brainstorm: The Power and Purpose of the Teenage Brain.* New York: Penguin Group.

Tough, Paul (2012). *How Children Succeed: Grit, Curiosity and the Hidden Power of Character.* New York: Houghton Mifflin Harcourt Publishing Company.

Truman, Karol Kuhn (2003) *Feelings Buried Alive Never Die.*
St. George, Utah: Olympus Distributing. Gottman as
referenced in Hall. P30.

Watkins, John 1971 'Inventor of the Affect Bridge'
EMDR lecture. Russel quoting Stickgold (2014), Seattle,
WA.Magazine Reference: Interpersonal Neurobiology:
New Horizons for Christian Counseling Christian Coun-
seling Today, vol. 20; no 3. Gary Sibcy, Tim Clinton, and
Ron Hawkins. (2014).

CPSIA information can be obtained
at www.ICGtesting.com
Printed in the USA
FFHW010622230419
51524635-57334FF